Ultramarathon Mom

This book is dedicated to YOU, the Reader, whether a serious runner in search of tips for your first ultra, a weekend warrior thirsting for adventure, or an athlete-at-heart that needs some motivation to get back on track, there is something here for everyone, and although the stories are autobiographical, as you turn the pages I'd like you to blur out my image in your mind and visualize yourself in my shoes, living your own adventures and pushing your personal limits. Because anything anyone else can do, YOU can do, too.

HOLLY ZIMMERMANN

ULTRA MARATHON MOM

FROM THE SAHARA TO THE ARCTIC

Meyer & Meyer Sport

British Library Catalouging in Publication Data
A catalogue record for this book is available from the British Library

Ultramarathon Mom: From the Sahara to the Arctic
Maidenhead: Meyer & Meyer Sport (UK) Ltd., 2018
ISBN: 978-1-78255-139-3

Aachen, Auckland, Beirut, Cairo, Cape Town, Dubai, Hägendorf, Hong Kong, Indianapolis,
Manila, New Delhi, Singapore, Sydney, Tehran, Vienna

Credits
Design and Layout
Cover and Interior Design: Annika Naas
Layout: Amnet

Photos
Cover Photos:
© MARATHON DES SABLES 2016;
© www.Marathon-Photos.com

Interior Photos:
All photos © Holly Zimmermann,
unless otherwise noted

Editorial
Managing Editor: Elizabeth Evans

🕮 Member of the World Sports Publishers' Association (WSPA)
Printed by C-M Books, Ann Arbor, MI, USA
ISBN: 978-1-78255-139-3
Email: info@m-m-sports.com
www.m-m-sports.com

CONTENTS

CHAPTER 1

BAD MOM

One eye on the computer screen and the other on my son skating around on the ice. Just like every Monday and Friday afternoon I sat and watched my son's hockey practice, while simultaneously trying to get some editing work done.

Two women came and sat at the table next to me. One of them had a daughter in the same class as mine, and we exchanged greetings before she turned to the other woman and explained that I was the one who was soon going to run 250 kilometers through the Sahara Desert.

"Can you imagine? What if something happened to her?" she commented to her friend almost as if I weren't there. "She has four children! I would never do something like that!"

I was momentarily speechless. A near stranger was practically scolding me for being a bad mom. The thought that to take part in this race was irresponsible for a mother of four young children had never crossed my mind. Of course, I had considered the risks, as I do for anything in life, but to witness a reaction about my decision which was so opposite from my own was pretty eye-opening. I had to ask myself, *Am I really a bad mom? Was I putting my life unnecessarily at risk and in doing so jeopardizing the well-being of my children?*

The race at hand was the Marathon des Sables, a 257-kilometer (160 miles), seven-day stage race through the Moroccan Sahara. It was a fully self-sufficient event, meaning that everything you needed for the week, including clothing, food, sleeping bag, and any safety and personal items, must be carried with you the entire time. It was the 31st edition of the race, with over 1100 runners, 450 support staff, including 70 medical doctors, 120 all-terrain vehicles, two helicopters, a Cessna plane, four quad vehicles, and four camels, not to mention the group was protected by the Moroccan military which had an additional helicopter on site and significant ground presence.

We had a GPS tracker attached to our backpacks so we could not get lost, and even our family and friends at home could see where we were at all times, whether struggling over a sand dune, crossing a salt flat, or using the makeshift toilets in the camp.

That said, I was probably safer there than anywhere else on earth.

But still, I'd be away from my children for two weeks. I knew they'd be well taken care of because my in-laws would be with them during that time. But how much they would miss me, whether they would worry, have nightmares, or be proud and excited, I couldn't possibly know for sure beforehand. Though one thing I did know for certain was that this would be an adventure for all of us to remember.

CHAPTER 2

OUARZAZATE

It was midnight in Casablanca. The one-room departure hall for domestic flights was nearly full, and empty seats were sparse. Of course the two next to the crying baby were free, but I chose to stand against a wall where there was some quiet. A crossroads between Europe and Africa, the cultures, clothing, and languages came from all over and provided entertainment in the form of people-watching for the couple hours layover.

Then my husband, Frank, and I snapped up a small dirty table by the kiosk that was just being vacated by a couple of men. A cold can of beer provided a small amount of relief to the hours of waiting.

A voice from behind me interrupted my melancholy mood. "Are you Holly?"

"Yes," I answered the stranger, a little surprised. "How do you know me?"

"I recognize you from your photos...in your blog."

His yellow Marathon des Sables (MdS) backpack gave him away as another runner on his way to Ouarzazate. We welcomed him to join us, and he recalled tales of his two previous races through the Moroccan Sahara. "Last year I had to walk most of it. I had a fractured femur," he said.

I was tired. We were all tired. The conversation was only mildly entertaining, and we had no information on the flight.

Suddenly, the sign above one of the gates lit up, announcing a flight to Tangier. Most of the passengers in the room began to line up. Something didn't seem right. Why was everyone boarding? Were we flying alone to Ouarzazate?

We didn't recall any flight announcements, but we may have just missed them in our fog of fatigue.

Frank asked one of the attendants controlling the room. "Yes. This flight. Ouarzazate," was the answer in almost unrecognizable English. The attendants then started yelling, "Ouarzazate! Here!" And most of the remaining travelers in the room got into the line as well.

After nodding in and out of sleep, an hour and a half later we landed at our final destination, Ouarzazate, the last outpost before the Sahara and the meeting point for the Marathon des Sables.

It was almost 3am by the time we collapsed exhausted into a pristinely-pillowed, king-size bed in Le Berbere Palace, a beautiful western-style hotel, which would serve as our oasis for the next few days.

The room was pitch dark (due to the heavy drapes) when the ringing of Frank's phone woke us at 8:30 am. A business call that he didn't answer.

We'd missed dinner the night before, and I was starving. So despite the urge to roll over and go back to sleep, we got up for breakfast. Oh, that Moroccan mint tea! Beans for protein. Corn cakes for carbohydrate. Canned fruit...to play it safe. There was also plenty of fresh fruit and squeezed juices, but I needed to be careful. Stomach trouble had the potential of turning months of training and preparation into a *fruitless* exercise. I'd been in Morocco before and gotten sick on something that had me hugging the porcelain bowl in my hotel for two days. The general rule in most African nations, as well as many countries in South America and Asia, is to only eat fruits or vegetables that have been peeled, thoroughly washed, or cooked. Many travelers avoid salads altogether. No point in taking the risk.

Time to acclimate. Bikini. Pool. Not really sure how long we lay there. An hour? Two? It didn't matter. We had no schedule to keep, no one to account for except ourselves. We travel only occasionally without the kids, so having to answer only to our own needs and desires was a rare luxury—though I did send them some photos via my mother-in-law, and I immediately got a text back from my son saying that he loves and misses me. Little heartbreaker.

We decided then it was time for a short jog to keep the muscles loose as well as check out the city. We'd been there 15 years earlier, when I was five months pregnant with our first child, and we quickly noticed that not much had changed except for a huge solar energy complex being built about six miles outside of town.

We had arrived on Monday, and the buses for the runners were scheduled to depart for basecamp for the 31st Marathon des Sables on Friday morning, which is also when Frank was scheduled to fly home. There was no place for spectators on the course, so it made no sense for him to stay in Morocco, but it was nice to spend a few days together in pure relaxation while trying to get used to the climate before the start

Text from my nine-year-old Robert via Oma's cell phone

of the race. Although, it was not as hot as I'd expected it to be. I don't think it was even over 30 °C (86 °F). How could I acclimate in that? But it was dry. Very dry. So much so that my throat and bronchia were irritated, and my nose was bleeding a little. But these symptoms were gone after a few days. Good enough to mentally justify my "acclimation phase" in the lap of luxury.

The first night in Ouarzazate we ate at Chez Dimitri, which is supposed to be one of the best restaurants in the city. It is not fancy but known for its high-quality and delicious local food. The walls are decorated with photos of their well-known clientele, mostly actors and actresses who have eaten there while shooting

Chez Dimitri: The best restaurant in town

at the film studios on the outskirts of the city. A photo of Hillary Clinton hung prominently over our table.

While enjoying the vegetable tagine, I noticed another table with two men who were speaking English and were clearly American. Bits and pieces of their conversation told me that they were also here for the MdS, so when we got up to leave, I stopped by at their table to say hello.

Turns out they were both veterans of the race, and one of them was the coordinator for the American runners. I couldn't believe my luck at meeting him since I was interested in getting an American tent assignment. These assignments were not very strict, but normally allocated by country of residence, and since I live in Germany, I would be expected to be in with the Germans,

Austrians, and Swiss—the German-speaking contingent. There were eight people to a tent, whereby the term "tent" at the MdS has a very different definition than what many of us think of when camping. This was not exactly a cozy little wind-and-weather-proof nylon home nestled among beautiful pine trees in front of a crackling campfire.

Wipe that image off the slate.

What we have in the desert are Berber-style tents, which are essentially rudimentary shelters with a large fabric cover of black burlap held up by uneven wooden poles of varying length and thickness. Two of the longer poles hold up the middle, and four shorter poles hold up the four corners. On the floor is one huge handwoven carpet. Home sweet home.

Berber-style tent used for the Marathon des Sables in Morocco
© MARATHON DES SABLES 2016

My initial thoughts were that a US tent, surrounded by my own language and childhood culture, might make me feel more at home, especially when I am in a state of physical exhaustion. I mentioned that to the coordinator, and he said, yes, he did have a spot in one of the tents! He took my name and contact info. I was thrilled and relieved. And so was my husband who would be leaving prior to me heading out into no-man's land; now he felt reassured that I would be in good hands.

We left the restaurant with full stomachs, light-headed from the local white wine, and feeling content. We strolled through the summer festival that was in full swing. Teenagers (well, teenage boys) were dancing to the band playing music on stage; stalls were open, selling everything from handicrafts, to shoes, popcorn, pastries, and soaps. We talked briefly with many of the shopkeepers, but with one we lingered longer than the others because his English was pretty good. He told us about where he came from in the mountains and that he was there to sell some of the handcrafts of his people. He then asked us if we had some medicine that we could give him. He wanted nothing specific, just anything that we could spare to help the people in his village. I apologized because I had nothing. Really nothing. Not only because I was traveling light because of the race, but also because I don't use medicine unless it is absolutely necessary. He said he understood and knew of the race that I was about to embark on, so we talked about that shortly before moving on.

My long hair was flowing freely, but in an Islamic-dominated country, I was careful to cover my arms and legs with clothing out of respect for the culture of those who live there. We passed by a tent full of women and young girls who were selling pastries. They seemed to be charmed by me and called me into their stall. I couldn't resist. To Frank's surprise, I sat down, and they immediately brought me mint tea and offered me something to eat. We began to communicate in English on a very basic level, but we mostly just giggled. The international language of women.

As we left the festival and walked back to the hotel, it began to get windy, and trash was blowing all around. I didn't sleep well that night. A storm had kicked up, and the wind was ferocious. During a short jog upon waking the next morning, it had me blowing all over the place. A bridge with a strong crosswind made me feel that each time I lifted my foot to take a step, it landed inches away from where I'd intended to plant it.

The temperature was cooler, too. How could I get use to the heat if there was none? My solution: a hamam. The hamam is the Islamic variant of the Roman bath—a steamy sauna where you lie on hot stone benches and let every muscle relax before you get scrubbed and washed by an attendant and finally cooled down by buckets of fresh spring water. Oh, yes. It was heaven. Heavenly, dizzyingly hot. That was acclimation for sure.

Then a massage was called for, of course...for good measure.

A young girl brought me into a small, dimly-lit room and took my robe. An oil lamp stood in a corner. Dried flower petals lay in a bowl. I was asked to lie face down on the table, and she began to dry my hair which was wet from the hamam. Arabic music drifted softly about the room. Another woman entered, and they began whispering in French. The relaxation of body and mind was fully intoxicating.

An hour went by before I knew it, and I left the spa in an elevated state.

That afternoon we decided to try to find a new rug for our dining room. When we were in Morocco 15 years earlier, we had bought one that still lies under our dining table, but it was getting frayed on the edges, and we thought it would be nice to get a replacement from the same place, albeit Ouarzazate instead of Fez.

On our jogging jaunts through the city, we kept our eyes open for rug shops but didn't find much of anything, so we asked the concierge at our hotel. He picked up the phone and dialed; he spoke a few words in Arabic and then covered the mouthpiece and asked us when we wanted to go. Frank and I looked at each other in slight confusion…ah, when? Hmmm…how about in an hour?

The concierge said a few more words into the receiver, hung up, and told us that we would be picked up by a driver in an hour.

Now that's service!

Well, Moroccan-style service.

The driver who picked us up was severely physically handicapped— my guess was a battle with childhood polio—and the car was most certainly older than I am…and I am not young. There were no seat belts, and one of the rear doors did not open. But as the spirit of this trip was adventure, it kept with the theme.

We were whisked away, down into and through the city and then back out the other side and up some narrow streets full of potholes and clouds of dust before we parked across the street from a large building with an intricately carved gate around an entrance surrounded by a beautiful assortment of green pottery and a giant black camel carved out of wood.

We had arrived at the Labyrinthe du Sud.

Our welcoming party immediately came out—a rotund man in flowing white robes and a cobalt blue turban.

Our welcoming party at the Labyrinthe du Sud

The front room was dark as we entered, but with the flick of a switch, warm light glowed from shimmering, mirrored lamps.

It was the *Nights of Arabia*, the *Queen of Sheba*, and *Raiders of the Lost Ark* all in one. From floor to ceiling were handcrafted tables, pottery, mirrors, jewelry, cooking devices, swords, saddlery, instruments, and furniture. I would need a week just to look at everything in the room! But there was more…another room adjacent was full of jewelry, and through another door, vibrantly colorful handwoven rugs were stacked to the rafters.

We were guided through the rooms and given brief descriptions of the most beautiful and interesting items. It was like a private tour of a lost museum full of treasures. I had my eye on several things, but Frank was anxious to get down to business, so we moved into the rug room and explained what we were looking for. Two helpers were standing by but darted off after a few words of Arabic from their boss. In an instant they were back and proceeded to spread out an amazing rug before us…an incredible plush candy-apple red that I just wanted to roll around on and then curl up into. I was amazed that I loved the very first rug that I saw, so I hoped that there would be much more to come. So many different colors and styles, from the Middle East, the Far East, and everywhere in between. I was overwhelmed. But, the first one was my favorite from the 20 or 30 that we looked at. Unfortunately, it was too small and too cozily-thick to be a dining room rug. After we'd seen enough, we sat and drank mint tea over negotiations, and after three hours we headed out with our purchases: a patchwork-style rug perfect for my office, some jewelry for our daughters and a knife for our son, and although the frayed rug from Morocco 2001 still lies under our dining room table, the candy-apple red looks gorgeous in my bedroom.

After being "chauffeured" back to our hotel, we decided to take a walk downtown, find a café, and have a drink to celebrate our purchases. But we soon found out that the cafés near the Kasbah Taourirt had no liquor licenses, so we headed toward the newer part of town and stumbled upon a building that looked like a restaurant. We ascended the front stairs and took one step inside the door, whereby we were immediately approached by a young man who blocked our path and asked what we wanted. Frank told him that we wanted to sit on the terrace. We could hear the sounds of a crowd inside, though as we looked into the main room there was not a soul to be seen. The man told us that they had no food. Frank replied that we just wanted to drink a beer and asked again if they had a terrace. Yes, downstairs, the man replied. I was a little nervous and skeptical, so I told Frank he could go check it out while I waited outside. He followed the man and soon disappeared down a dark narrow staircase.

A minute later he returned with excitement etched on his face. "Come, you have to see this," he said. I followed him down into the dungeon and was surprised at what I saw (and the fact that Frank thought it would be great for me to see it). It was a very dark room, a bar, filled with dozens of people. As my eyes adjusted to the light I realized that I was the only woman present. And all eyes were on me. The man then pointed to the "terrace," a small dirty slab of concrete out back loaded with junk. Frank looked at me with anticipation. "Don't even think about it," I answered and marched right out of that place.

With our hopes of getting a beer fading, we decided to change plans when we saw a pharmacy. We went in and asked for some painkillers, gauze, Band-Aids, and eye drops. The pharmacist was skeptical at first, but when we told her the medicine was to be given to someone who would bring it to villagers in the mountains, she became very helpful.

By that time, it was almost 6pm, and we were hungry and thirsty. We headed back to Chez Dimitri, as it was good the night before, and there were really not many other options around. He was officially closed but let us in and gave us a beer and olives while we waited. Pure heaven.

It was cool and windy, so the front door was kept shut, but every time someone entered or exited a gust of cold air blew in, and I was chilled. There were very few customers that night. Where was everyone? I figured that runners would start flooding into the city by now, but not even our American friends showed up.

After dinner we headed back to the festival, but it was quiet because of the wind and cold. A few shopkeepers recognized us from the night before. I smiled and waved. We saw the man from the shop who had asked us for medicine to bring to his people in the mountains. He invited us to sit with him, and he ordered tea. We then offered him the items that we'd bought from the pharmacy. He opened the bag and looked inside, took out a couple of items, and examined them. He did not seem happy. He explained that the medicine from Europe is better, stronger, and that's why he had asked us if we had anything from home that we could spare. I began to explain again how I was here for the race and had only a small suitcase with a few things. But why did I feel bad? We just gave him medicine that was surely needed by him, his family, and others in his village. *"Beggars can't be choosers"* ran through my mind, but I knew the culture here was different, and we did the only thing we could.

We drank more tea and chatted about the festival, the weather, and the race. He said that last year a French woman came into his shop before the race and bought a necklace that she wore while running, and subsequently placed third overall. I knew this wasn't true as I'd studied previous results. He then showed us some necklaces, and one caught my eye—a pinkish-brown stone with a few silver beads. He said the stone was coral. Coral in the desert, we asked? He said that it used to be a sea here, which we'd known, though it was hard to believe. The coral seemed very symbolic to me, since I grew up near the ocean. We asked the price, and he immediately switched to his salesman mode. He took out an ancient scale and placed the necklace on one arm with small lead counterweights on the other. He asked Frank for a Dirham because the necklace didn't quite match the counterweight. I was hoping the Dirham was the price of the piece of jewelry, but he wasn't finished yet with his charade. Next he took out an ancient-looking leather-bound book full of handwritten Arabic notes. He looked back at the necklace and again pointed to the silver (silver-looking?) beads before he told us the price was 1,050 Dirham (about 100 Euros, or $118 US). Frank got up without saying anything and walked out. He was angry. I was very disappointed. I was more than willing to pay a fair price but was slightly offended when I thought he was trying to take advantage of us. He asked Frank what he thought a fair price would be. Frank answered, 100 Dirham. I thought this was probably low, but the necklace certainly didn't appear to be all that valuable. Now the dealer seemed offended. We knew this game from our afternoon at the rug shop as well as from our previous travels, but we were tired and wanted to go back to the hotel, with or without the necklace. He then asked me for a fair price. I told him a maximum of 150 Dirham. He scoffed. I moved to leave, and he called me back again. He gestured to the medicine and asked what it cost. I told him it was a gift and had nothing to do with the necklace. It is their culture to negotiate, but I was too tired. I just told him the truth. I said that I like the necklace, but I don't *need* it, and if he can sell it to someone else at that price, then it is ok with me. He should keep it and earn his money. He asked again for a "final fair" price, and I told him 150. He held out his hand to shake on the deal. He said he was happy. Am I happy, he asked? Yes, I said. Though, was I? Not really. Negotiating feels like arguing to me, and it leaves an unpleasant feeling in its wake. But I did end up wearing the necklace for the entire race, and I am certain it gave me good luck while crossing the ancient seabed.

The next day, after our morning run and breakfast, we decided to take a tour of the film studio located on the outskirts of Ouarzazate. We hailed a taxi outside of our hotel for the short ride.

Atlas Studios was located just on the edge of the city, and parts of *Lawrence of Arabia* and *Gladiator* as well as some episodes of *Game of Thrones* were filmed there. But to the innocent bystander it doesn't

"Happy" with my coral necklace from the bazaar

look like much of anything at all. At least you could say it is very different from the Hollywood film studios with all their glitz and glamour. Atlas Studios is set in a huge expanse of desert and mountains, spotted with some interesting buildings made to look like Egyptian temples or middle-eastern city streets. After the hour-long tour, we went into the hotel located on the premise and ordered two espressos in the café and then began to observe the people. It was very international, with apparent actors, actresses, directors, and others in the film business. There was currently a shoot for a cooking show going on, but everything seemed so chaotic and disorganized that it was hard to make sense of anything. Chalk it up as another adventure.

That night we decided to eat dinner at the hotel. I ordered Moroccan soup as an appetizer after specifically asking if it contained meat. The waiter said it did not. But once I started to eat, I realized that it did. I'd given up meat a few years before and knew if I ate it now, I probably wouldn't be able to digest it, so I pushed it aside. But I certainly didn't go hungry because for the main course I ordered couscous with veggies, and it was enough to feed four people. Seriously. I ate for what seemed an eternity, and when I couldn't stuff anything more in, the waiter cleaned it away even though it looked as though it hadn't been touched.

It was Wednesday night. I only had one more full day in the safe haven of the hotel and the company of my husband before I'd be bused out into the desert for nine days.

The anticipation was building. And I was getting nervous.

CHAPTER 3

BEATRICE

Pigeons flew low over the pool and swooped in along the surface to catch a drink of water. The bright blue of the tiles reflected on the undersides of their wings, giving them the appearance of tropical birds. An optical illusion turning the ordinary into the exotic. The irony could not be overlooked: We were ordinary people about to embark on an extraordinary adventure.

There were so few guests at the hotel that week that Frank and I essentially had our regular spots at the pool every day—two lounge chairs with a table in the middle and an umbrella—and next to us was always the same French couple (who I'd see later at the MdS). That was essentially the sum total of the pool guests except for random visitors who ate lunch at the outdoor bar.

But today, Thursday, the day before the official departure for the MdS, the city was starting to come alive. Apparently, a large group of guests had arrived at 3:00 in the morning, the concierge had told us. There was a long table set up on the garden terrace full of envelopes with Italian names on them. Could they be runners? I spotted a couple of MdS backpacks on newcomers to the pool area. I was hopeful, but then there was a sign in the lobby for the insurance company, AXA. Drat.

The afternoon sun was hot, so we lay in the shade of the umbrella. Beatrice was supposed to meet us there soon. The MdS organizer for the German-speaking participants had put me in contact with her a few weeks earlier. At the time I wondered why the organizer couldn't just help Beatrice with her arrangements on her own, but now that I know Beatrice, I understand. She is a very special case and much too much for the organizer to handle by herself.

A spicy little 49-year-old beauty, she runs a fashion blog and has an aura the size of Texas. She was born and raised in Italy, later working as a bond broker in London, before finally settling down to have a family in Zurich, Switzerland. Though "settling down" is just a figure of speech because this woman never stops, not for

a second. Anyway, we had exchanged emails for the past couple of weeks about travel, hotels, and basics about the race. Since both of us have blogs, we knew a little about each other beforehand and were sure to recognize each other from our photos. But I was still overwhelmed when we first met.

Beatrice looking glamorous (Note: She looked almost as good as this after nine days in the desert without showering.)
© Beatrice Lassi

She came right up to Frank and me at the hotel pool, hardly giving the French couple a look, even though I thought the French woman and I looked similar, and she began to chat away, with me hardly able to get a word in. She said she didn't have a bathing suit with her; I offered one of mine, but she declined and proceeded to strip down to her bra and running shorts. Regardless of there being no pool guests to complain, no one would have said a word anyway since she possessed an insanely gorgeous body. How old are you really, Beatrice? 49 or 29?

We talked a little about our gear for the race and how much our packs weighed. Mine was about 7 kilograms (15 pounds); she told me she wasn't certain, but at last weigh-in hers was about 10 kilograms (22 pounds), though it could be more now. I was shocked. She is a tiny little woman; there was no way she'd be able to lug that much over 250 kilometers! She then begged me for help since she really wasn't at all sure of what she actually needed to bring and what she could leave behind. The three of us decided to head down to Beatrice's hotel, get her stuff organized, and afterwards go to dinner together.

I had my Excel spreadsheet on hand which listed all my own gear broken down into four categories: Mandatory Equipment, Clothing, Own Material, and Food (don't worry, I've included the full list in chapter 8 for your enjoyment).

Beatrice handed me her backpack. I plopped down on the bed, and we got to work. Frank and I are engineers, so we attacked the problem logically, step by step.

1. Get rid of all non-essential items.

I began to toss items into a pile on the side—a pile that was intended to stay behind. There was a huge gray-colored fleece jacket. A fully-loaded Swiss Army knife (typical Swiss). A knife was on the mandatory list for MdS race gear, but we kept instead the much lighter X-Acto knife which she also had in her pack. Tons of makeup. "No! I need my makeup!" she exclaimed. Frank and I laughed. She said that if she won't be able to shower for a week she at least needed some basic items. Even though she was without doubt the first and probably last woman competitor at the MdS to have makeup on hand, I knew that she wasn't going to budge on this, so we negotiated it down to two items that would accompany her across the Sahara. (Although I think she tucked more into her pack later when I had gone.)

That pile of non-essentials was fairly high by the end of the first step, and we were all pretty happy with ourselves, but the tough part was still to come.

2. Organize her food rations.

Beatrice had gone to a local sports store and told the guy there about the MdS. He loaded her up with all kinds of dehydrated camping meals, carbohydrate shakes, gels, and tubes of liquid protein. She had done her best to label the meals for each breakfast and dinner, but it was still not well organized into daily calorie and nutritional requirements. A minimum of 2,000 calories per day must be carried by each runner, and a spot check could be held at any time (so we were told, but to my knowledge they never do this). We got out our cell phone calculators and began putting together combinations of necessary energy and nutrient requirements for each day, starting by assigning the "heaviest" food items at the beginning of the week so that she could bring down the weight of the pack as soon as possible. Most of the gels were to stay behind as well as the liquid protein. They were too heavy, and they weren't really *food,* but rather simple calories. Although none of us would be eating gourmet that week, the desire to *chew* food and the mental satisfaction that it provides should not be underestimated. It was too late to go shopping, but at least I had some extra sports bars of my own on hand, so I supplemented her supplies with those. *Whew.*

3. Fit everything in the bag, and fit the bag to her.

Everything did not fit in the bag, but thankfully, unlike me, she hadn't cut off any of the straps on the outside, and we were able to attach her sleeping bag, mattress pad, and bright pink down jacket (she would not part with it) on the outside of her bag. Then we made sure that it was adjusted to her tiny little body, but didn't squish her large breasts. (Yes, they are real. Some things in life are just not fair.)

We were finally finished. She was ready to go. And we were all starving. We headed out to Dimitri's once again for a meal. The owner greeted us warmly and gave us a bottle of wine, on the house. Two glasses, since Beatrice does not drink alcohol, but that doesn't stop her from chatting eternally without taking a breath. The stories she told us about her life were unbelievable, both shocking and hilarious, and by the time we said goodnight to her and left for our hotel, I was exhausted.

Once Frank and I were alone and down the road a bit I turned to him and said, "She is intense. I'm not sure if I am going to be able handle her for six hours on the bus tomorrow."

He laughed and agreed.

But I knew I'd found myself a friend.

CHAPTER 4

MDS DAY 1: CHECK-IN

FRIDAY, APRIL 8, LEAVE OUARZAZATE BY BUS AND ARRIVE AT BIVOUAC 1

7:00. Frank left the hotel for the airport to catch his flight home. I attempted to eat some breakfast but was not very hungry, so I packed my bags and tried not to think of what was to come.

8:00. I took a taxi to the Hotel La Gazelle to check in with the rest of the German-speaking contingent. Beatrice was already there and was scurrying around all corners of the breakfast room trying to get the best signal on the Wi-Fi. Last chance for the next nine days.

8:20. We boarded the buses to drive six hours to bivouac 1 (B1); at the time, we had no idea where it was. The exact course was not revealed to anyone beforehand, and it would be on the bus that we'd finally get the "Road

Map," which had the course map and description. So, essentially, we put ourselves completely in the hands of the organization. Faith in our fellow man and woman.

10:00. I had to pee so badly I was in agony. I tried to avoid drinking too much that morning, and normally I don't have troubles like this, but it was an emergency. So I requisitioned Beatrice to help. It was turning out to be a blessing in disguise having her there! She got up and went to the front of the bus to use her charm and talk to the volunteers in charge. A minute later she came back with bad news. We were one of six buses; if we stopped, the whole entourage had to stop; try to hold it until noon. No way! There was going to be an accident here very soon. But then, about ten minutes later, the volunteer came back and announced that we would make a quick stop. Internal jubilation! And wouldn't you know it, everyone on all those six buses piled out of the vehicles as quickly as they could—men on the right side of the road, women on the left—and emptied their bladders into the hot Sahara sand.

12:00. Lunch stop. Same scenario as before, whereby hundreds of runners hurriedly exited the buses to relieve themselves. What had everyone been drinking? We received a bag lunch and sat on the hard, rocky ground to eat. There was a little of everything in that bag: bread, fruit, packaged cheese and meat (gave that away), couscous salad, and orange juice. At the time, it seemed pretty ordinary, but when we received that same type of bag lunch on our return bus ride after spending nine days in the desert and eating out of our backpacks, well then, it was a feast fit for a king!

Six busloads of runners make a potty break in the Sahara.

15:00. The buses pulled off the dirt road onto hard-packed ground. The two buses in the front continued driving farther into the desert, while the other four, including the bus that Beatrice and I were on, stayed behind. We were allowed outside where we were told that only two buses at a time could continue the last kilometer so that there was not a mad rush to check into the tents. Half an hour later, our bus was allowed to drive on.

15:30. We had arrived at B1. I checked into the American tent, but it was very crowded with eight people. I was shown a narrow space in the middle which was to be my home for the duration. I began chatting with the other members but immediately felt uncomfortable. They were telling tales about their past ultras: Badwater (135 miles nonstop through Death Valley), 100-mile races, and jungle marathons. What had I done? A few single-stage ultras of no more than 70 kilometers (43 miles). I was beginning to feel insecure. I then decided to go for a walk and check out the rest of the camp, and I soon came across Beatrice. There were only four people assigned to her tent. She suggested I join them. I was relieved. So I switched to the Swiss tent....my home for the next nine days! The other members of our tent included Mike from Zurich, our only Swiss man in a Swiss tent, and the other two were from Brazil, a father and son pair, Cap (our captain) and Fernando, his son. Cap, the patriarch, still lives in Brazil, and his English was rudimentary, but Fernando had lived outside of Zurich for a few years and had also run the MdS before. Our tent language was then, conveniently enough for me, English! Many other tents hung out their country flags, but since we were such a mix we decided to hang out one of Beatrice's bras instead. This made it easy for us to find our tent out of the 166 in concentric rings that all looked alike; it also got a lot of attention ...and a lot of laughs.

Our tent flag, a.k.a. Beatrice's sacrificial bra

17:00. Beatrice and I went on a walk to check out the layout of the tent village and also to find the ladies' room. Of course, there was no ladies' room, and on that first day we shyly walked as far as possible away from the ring of tents to empty our bladders, but during the following days, that trek to find a spot to pee got shorter and shorter. There was no point in being shameful; we were all in the same boat.

Then Beatrice spotted two helicopters at the edge of the camp. She wanted to go in and take a closer look, so we wandered toward them and soon saw three men (not runners) standing in a group next to one of the machines. I stopped at a safe distance, but Beatrice wanted to go and talk (i.e., flirt) with them. As we approached, two of the men, who appeared to be some of the local support staff, humbly walked away, but one man remained. "Are you the pilot?" Beatrice asked. He responded affirmatively with a

Beatrice making friends with the helicopter pilot

big smile. Beatrice continued to make small talk with a now very happy pilot, and after a few photos we were on our way again.

18:00.   We noticed a cameraman who was filming some of the other runners. Beatrice and I both agreed that he should be filming us instead. We started talking to him, and he asked if he could come back to our tent and do short interviews with us, which thus started a relationship that lasted throughout the week. No, not that kind of a relationship!

We brought cameraman Arnaud back to our Tent 40 and introduced him to the other guys. Arnaud was enthralled with Cap and Fernando, and after shooting short interviews with Beatrice and me, he asked to shoot father and son. During the following days he kept coming back to film short updates on Cap and Fernando until he had filmed a week-long project. They truly made a great story. Fernando had run the race the previous year

Cameraman Arnaud

and had done quite well. After recalling the fascinating stories of his MdS adventures to his family, Fernando's father decided that he, too, wanted to take part, but since he was not a runner, the two decided to walk. The father and son team walked the entire 257 kilometers, side by side.

19:00. Dinner in the bivouac! Dinner on Friday as well as breakfast, lunch, and dinner on Saturday were provided by the organization. We sat on the ground and ate around low tables. Vermicelli with cinnamon and raisins. Oven-roasted vegetables. Bread. Endless bottles of water. Once the race started we would be responsible for all our own meals and would not even have the luxury of eating from a low table.

Dinner at the bivouac on arrival day

20:00. It was now dark and getting cold, so everyone got into their sleeping bags. For two hours we listened while the occupants of one of the British tents behind us inflated four giant double-bed air mattresses to be used the first two nights in the bivouac; two final nights of sleeping comfortably! This was a little disheartening while I lay on the hard, cold ground with no mattress at all! Once we would leave B1, the Brits would simply abandon the mattresses for the locals because they would be too heavy and large to carry in their backpacks.

I wasn't very tired, so I just lay there in a blanket of anxiety, letting doubt run through my head. Did I have enough experience? Had I trained enough? Was I really prepared for this?

CHAPTER 5

TRAINING FOR THE MARATHON DES SABLES

I admit it. At the beginning I was completely naïve as far as training for a race of that magnitude. Running more than 250 kilometers in a week is difficult enough in an optimal environment, but through the desert with 15 pounds of gear on my back? I had no personal coach at the time to guide me, but with the plethora of information on the Internet and my ever-growing pile of running books, I knew that I could educate myself well enough in the 15 months between when I registered for the MdS and the race start to run it like a pro. I figured my training would be multifaceted. Naturally, endurance would be the key, and I would achieve that through long runs, long-distance biking, back-to-back (-to-back) long runs, long hikes, combination training comprised of long runs, long bike rides, and long hikes, and uh, did I mention long runs? See a recurring theme here? All that would be fortified by strength work, sand-specific and other specialized training, and acclimatization.

My plan was that a typical training week would contain these elements:

- Long runs, 25-plus kilometers (1X)
- Interval training (0-1X, meaning that some weeks would be without intervals, but other weeks they would occur once)
- Tempo runs (1X)
- Regeneration runs (1X)
- Mid-long runs, 15-25 kilometers (1-2X)
- Long bike (1-2X)
- Strength training (3X)
- Yoga/Stretching (3X)
- Hill work (0-1X)
- Drills (0-2X)
- Special sessions (sand, sauna, weighted backpack, etc.) (0-2X)
- Day off! (0-1X) :)

Exactly where those items fell was not something that I wanted to specifically plan far in advance (though obviously there had to be some structure and sensibility in terms of order of appearance). I had the mornings free when the kids were in school and could juggle the workouts as needed. Flexibility is key for me as there are always "uncontrollable factors," such as a sick child, weather, vacation, appointments, kids' birthday parties, and so on. All had their varying influence on my training schedule. My first priority was (and is) my family, and then if those workouts made their regular appearances, I would be happy.

I had a basic plan to build mileage (*kilometerage?*) over that year, and although most plans build for three weeks before having a week of regeneration, I find that that occurs naturally in my training due to those "uncontrollable factors." In the end it all comes out in the wash.

The year prior to the race was subdivided into trimesters highlighted by key events. The first event was the Regensburg

Half Marathon in the middle of May. This race was not critical in terms of my performance, but I wanted to be in pretty good shape for it and possibly qualify for the New York City Marathon. The only "hindrance" during that period was a trip to Nepal with my family over Easter. During that trip, long runs were going to be all but non-existent, so I had to focus on strength training and speed or hill work (think, Himalayas).

The second key race in the schedule was the Regensburg Landkreislauf Ultramarathon in September, prior to which I had a multitude of other events, including a few 10Ks, another half marathon, and bike races. An important training event during this period was a weekend in Switzerland at the beginning of August, a trail running camp, in which the agenda was to run with a small group with full backpacks 80 kilometers (50 miles) over two-and-a-half days with 5,000 meters (16,000 feet) positive elevation. The weekend was organized by two men who had run the Marathon des Sables before, so I was planning on picking them clean for info.

Then at the end of August, I was in Mallorca for a week. Again, a family vacation, but I figured I could get in several long runs there as well as some sand training. Yahoo! But the week after that I was going to be on a cruise ship in the Mediterranean with my family and in-laws, who invited us to celebrate their 50th wedding anniversary with them. My father-in-law excitedly told me how they allow guests to use one of the upper decks to run laps in the early morning. At first I was optimistic, until I learned it would be 10 laps for one kilometer. Ah, wonderful. I was dizzy at the thought of it. But the ship had a great fitness room and offered an infinite schedule of aerobics and spinning classes. So, I thought I'd be ok.

The third segment of my training plan was over the winter, comprising the last six months leading up to the MdS. This was also obviously the real buildup of endurance, gradually increasing my mileage each week. I had also planned to combine it with long "hikes," i.e., walking (how boring!), but I thought it would be necessary since the terrain in the desert is not always run-able. I would also be wearing the weighted backpack more frequently on middle-distance runs. In addition, running in the snow with shoe chains would provide invaluable strength training. Not to mention, I planned to spend time in the sauna—either on the bike trainer (at 40 °C, 100 °F) or simply sweating it out (90 °C, 200 °F)!

So that was the basic plan. Multifaceted training broken down into three segments highlighted by two milestone races and beginning with basic training.

FIRST TRIMESTER TRAINING

Just like in pregnancy, the first trimester can be a beast in disguise! The nausea, fatigue, sleepless nights, and endless worrying. And so it was with my first trimester training for the Marathon des Sables …well, except for the nausea.

Despite our best intentions, life loves to throw its curve balls, and you never know when one of them is going to bonk you on the head. My first major knock was already underway when I registered for the MdS as I was sick with some kind of wild virus that was running rampant through Regensburg, Germany (where I live). I tried to train but was constantly set back and was more or less out of commission for eight weeks; this wasn't such a bad thing in itself as it forced me to take a maybe-not-so-unneeded break for my body, though my psychological well-being suffered. Then, finally, at the beginning of March, I was ready to go again in full force and really was making some good progress until our planned family vacation in Nepal over the Easter holiday.

Do I plan my vacations around my workouts and races? Honestly, no. But once the dates and locations are set, I start considering my training options (and whether there just happens to be a cool race in the area while there). Some people think this is nuts (well, a lot of people think that about me anyway...so who cares!), but I love sports, and a vacation without exercise is just not for me. I try not to let it impact our family time together, and sometimes I get up at the crack of dawn to get it done. I don't need much, but an hour or two a day makes me a more balanced and happy person—not only good for me, but also good for the people around me.

Some destinations are easy. Miles of running, biking, and hiking routes in the mountains or on the beach; a hotel with aerobics classes, fitness studio, a lap pool, or even tennis courts, and your workouts are fun. But other destinations are not so easy. Enter: Nepal.

My husband and I decided to schlep our four kids to Nepal for 12 days—some cultural sightseeing in Kathmandu (a reality-check for our spoiled beloved children), a little hiking in paradise, and a jungle safari to top it off.

But I knew Nepal would be a difficult place to get in some long-distance running, though I was hoping for some decent fitness centers and swimming pools to fill in the gaps (unfortunately disappointed by both). Here's what I ended up with.

Sign posted on a tree in the gardens of our hotel in Dhulikhel, Nepal

HOLLY'S TRAINING LOG: NEPAL

Day 1: After 24 hours of travel door to door, the only sport I was doing was lifting a cocktail glass to my lips and then hopping into bed.

Day 2: Five-kilometer run on 400-meter "track" (quaint path) in the garden of my hotel in Kathmandu. I was the only runner, but there were several middle-aged Nepali men walking who were rather amused at my presence. Thirty minutes of strength training in the hotel gym.

Day 3: Thirty minutes of strength training. Forty minutes of fartlek running on treadmill in hotel gym (sporadically disrupted by power outages).

Day 4: One-hour yoga class at hotel in Dhulikhel. One hour of yogi-instructor-led meditation. (You think that's not sport? Give it a try.)

Day 5: Two-hour easy hike with family. One hour of yoga. Climbing a bazillion steps at the hotel.

Day 6: A 20-kilometer trail run in the Himalayan foothills (sounds like a dream, but it really happened, and you can read all about it if you make it to the bottom of this list).

Day 7: Rest (8-hour drive to Pokhara; not actually restful, though beautiful and eye-opening).

Day 8: Ran 4 kilometers up the mountain to coffee house (strongest cup of joe ever!). Thirty minutes strength training. Two-hour easy hike with family. One hour of rowing my *lazy* beautiful daughter across the lake. Two-hour yoga class.

Day 9: Rest (6-hour drive to Chitwan National Park. Note: ride from hell in a van with a Nepalese driver—more potholes than asphalt, hairpin curves on cliffs with no guardrail, accidents, animals, and daredevil speeds).

Day 10: Forty-five minutes of lap swimming.

Day 11: Five-kilometer run around hotel grounds with 5 x 200-meter accelerations plus 30 minutes of strength training.

Day 12: Elephant polo! (At least the elephant got a workout). The toughest part for me was trying to stay on the animal as it ran back and forth across the field. The elephants knew exactly what they were doing and seemed to really enjoy the game!

Me giving elephant polo a try

That was basic maintenance at best, and I had to be creative, but I was satisfied with it. For some more ideas about keeping in shape while on vacation, check out the appendix of this book.

MY HEAVENLY TRAIL RUN IN NEPAL

When planning our trip to Nepal, I just couldn't resist the idea of going on a long trail run in the Himalayan foothills. Visions of idyllic villages, colored by prayer flags, along long-forgotten paths set on a back-drop of the snow-covered Himalayas....ah, yes, that's what I had in mind.

But I couldn't just get-up-and-go by myself, into the wilderness, not knowing my way around. Plus, as a woman, well, I just don't feel comfortable running alone for long in unknown territory. Therefore, I needed a guide. But how would I organize something like that from halfway around the world? I mean, how could I find someone in rural Nepal who would be willing to run for more than a couple of hours with me? Where there's a will, there's a way.

Prior to leaving, I had done some internet searching, Facebooking, and emailing, and eventually after a few tips, I found Kyaron, a trail runner who would guide me on a two- to three-hour run in the Himalayan foothills.

Kyaron is an enthusiastic Nepalese trail runner, nature enthusiast, and environmentalist who lives in Nagarkot, not far from Dhulikhel where my family and I would be spending a few days during our 12-day tour of the country. When I first contacted him, his reaction to my request was circumspect, for obvious reasons. *What kind of a crazy lady is this?* But after he had a look at my webpage, he realized that I was serious, and we got down to the business of planning. Since I was with my whole family on vacation, I didn't want to spend too much time away, but I did want to make the adventure worthwhile, so we planned a round-trip, 20-kilometer run from my hotel in Dhulikhel up to the largest Tibetan Buddhist Monastery in Nepal: Thrangu Tashi Yangtse. The monastery is located at the sacred pilgrimage site of Namo Buddha. Despite its rural location, it is home to more than 250 monks and includes a monastic college, a school for young monks, and a Tibetan medical clinic.

I wasn't sure what to expect in terms of terrain difficulty, and I figured elevation would certainly come into play. At home we are less than 400 meters above sea level, whereas Dhulikhel was at about 1,700 meters, and we were to have another 1,000 meters of positive elevation over the course of the run itself. Would I be out of breath after the first kilometer? Would the dust stifle me? Will I have enough water in my hand-held bottle if I don't have a chance to buy some more? And, of course…could I trust this guy? I told my husband that if I was not back after four hours to call in the guards.

But when Kyaron met me at my hotel, I knew from the first moment that I was in good hands. He has a kind face, a warm smile, and though he has the look of a native Nepalese, his competent English made it clear that he has had ample Western influence, which became all the more obvious as he packed away his iPhone and tablet and left them with the hotel security.

After a minute or two of greeting, we were off, headed for the first challenge of the day: 1,000 steps up to a giant golden Buddha statue on a hill overlooking the world. But halfway up we had to slow to a walk; the elevation was rearing its ugly head. I was hoping this would not be foretelling of the rest of the day, and thankfully it was not. Once we got to the top, there was a refreshing downhill segment that wove through small villages and had some spectacular views of the valley. But I had to be really careful to keep my eyes on the ground as much as possible since the trail was extremely rough. And the weather cooperated. It was mostly sunny and dry with temps starting at a cool 15 °C (60 °F) and going up to about 25 °C (80 °F) by the time we finished.

At one point, upon entering a group of small huts, I looked ahead and saw a cow tethered to a fencepost on the side of the path. Then I heard the simple statement from Kyaron who was a step behind me, "A cow," and though I hardly knew him, his voice sounded odd, so I looked over at him and saw that he'd lost all color in his face. At the time, I didn't suspect much of anything and kept on running, right past the cow, but I didn't get far before I realized that Kyaron was no longer with me. I turned around to see that he hadn't made it past the animal and had a look of extreme apprehension. He was trying to get past the cow with as much distance between the two as possible. Finally, the cow moved off to one side, and Kyaron took the opportunity to dash by. He came back up next to me, and we continued running. He said nothing. I said nothing. But I couldn't help but wonder.

Soon after, an old woman emerged out of the bushes and began waving a curved knife at us. She had some kind of small trinket in her other hand and may have wanted to try to sell it to us, but I didn't stick around to find out. I bolted by her as fast as possible. Kyaron didn't seem bothered a bit.

After descending that first mountain, we had another long steep climb of about 5 kilometers up to the monastery, but it was much easier than the 1,000 steps to run, and we didn't need to stop. Our pace was moderate, and we talked about racing, nutrition, travel, and family. Just like any other running pair.

Once at the monastery, we took a short break and bought some bottled water. We then walked up to the main temple and took a look inside. It was breathtaking. Brilliantly colored fabrics draped the walls, hung from the ceiling, and lined the floors, prayer stools, and tables. A world away from the ornate gold-plated churches of Europe.

Outside we looked down upon a sports field where there must have been at least 50 young monks playing soccer and hacky sack, while others were just chasing each other around. Really no different than any other school yard in any other city in the world, except that they all had shaved heads and wore the same maroon-colored robes.

One of the monks we met near the temple who agreed to be photographed

We took the same route on the way back, though it looked completely new coming from the opposite direction (and we even took a couple of wrong turns...uhh, have you been here before Kyaron? Yes, yes, he replied). There were farmers everywhere tending their stepped fields; freshly-washed laundry was lying out on the grass to dry. And every time we passed through a group of houses, I couldn't help but smile at the surprised reactions on villager's faces when they saw me loping by in my brightly colored sports clothes and bouncing blond ponytail.

Freshly washed laundry set out to dry

Plenty of wildlife crossed our path along the way, including goats, chickens, and quite a few dogs, many of which tagged along and ran with us for varying distances. One dog even stayed right at my side for more than two kilometers. Kyaron reacted similarly to the dogs as he had with the cow. At one point, two dogs came running out onto the trail barking wildly at us. I simply ran by, not feeling threatened at all, but when I was past them, I turned around to see Kyaron at a standstill, shushing the dogs with a finger to his lips. Still puzzled by the cow incident, I asked him if he was afraid of dogs (as many people are), and he answered, "No. I like dogs." (Maybe one day you'll explain this to me, Kyaron?)

Shortly before descending the 1,000 steps to Dhulikhel, I stopped to take a closer look at the golden Buddha. We were required to take off our shoes before entering the monument, where I enjoyed the view and took a few photos. There was a group of Nepalese women taking pictures, and they were highly amused by my presence. "Hello! Hello!" they called out to me, laughing at their own use of the foreign greeting. Then one of them approached and wanted her photo taken with me. She stood so close, pushing herself into me, that I was afraid I was going to fall over the railing. And (ahem) I've just been running for two hours in the hot sun…how could anyone even bear to be that close to me at all?

Giant golden Buddha at the pinnacle of 1,000 steps

Back at the hotel, Kyaron met my family. We had a drink and a chat about the hotel and its history and significance (Dwarika's in Dhulikhel...truly Shangri-La). Then, before saying our goodbyes, I asked him if I could pay him a "guide fee," but he declined.

I guess it was as much as an adventure for him as it was for me. A run I'll never forget.

Namaste.

Sadly, 10 days after leaving Nepal, the country was brought to its knees by a series of earthquakes. It was hard to believe that the beautiful countryside and cities were in ruins, and the peaceful, happy people that we'd just met were now suffering beyond belief. At the time of the quake, Kyaron was hiking near the epicenter and was stranded for eight days before being helicoptered out. He then spent months helping others by distributing food and teaching water filtration methods in the

Kyaron and me

Kathmandu Valley. After that he went to China for nearly a year to study but is now back in Nepal fighting for environmental consciousness. He assures me the county has recovered well.

———————————

Back home from Nepal, I needed to take stock of my training for the MdS. Of course, other than my totally rockin' trail run with Kyaron in the Himalayan foothills, my training while there was basic maintenance at best. That said, in the middle of April (12 months prior to the MdS), I found myself in essentially the same condition I was back at the end of February.

What now? Three weeks until a 10K race and five until the Regensburg Half Marathon. I knew the best answer was as simple as could be: Be smart. Eat right. Train efficiently.

So, let's begin the eating part by playing a little game. I will give you two meal options, and you guess which is healthier. Ready? Go.

Starting with breakfast…

- Whole-grain cereal with milk **OR** Kale, pineapple, and nut smoothie
- Bagel with cream cheese **OR** Oatmeal with fresh berries
- A roll with liverwurst (German delicacy) **OR** Anything else

Lunch/Dinner…

- Pork chops and applesauce **OR** Black bean burger with mango chutney
- Pasta with fresh pesto **OR** Quinoa with grilled vegetables
- A Big Mac and extra-large fries **OR** Jumping off a bridge

So, how'd we do? I think it's pretty clear even to the untrained nutritionist. I knew that if I ate healthy meals but gorged on a bag of chips and a bar of chocolate every night, then I would not be doing myself any favors. Refined sugars and processed foods were also to be avoided as much as possible…doesn't take a rocket scientist.

The point is, that saying we learned in grade school is true: You are what you eat. Food *does* make a difference in how you feel, look, perform, smell (yes), and other, you know, minor things like life expectancy. And I really concentrated on putting healthy foods into my body (ahem, what about that wine and chocolate, Holly? Ok, ok, I'm only human, but everyone knows red wine and dark chocolate are loaded with antioxidants, so I could write those off *relatively* guilt free).

Of course, the next important part was training. I was beginning to have some great interval sessions and tempo runs, and my mileage was adding up. Then, just when I least expected it, I got whacked again by one of life's surprises. My husband, who'd been unwell since returning from Nepal, was getting sicker and sicker and subsequently had to be hospitalized due to high fever, dehydration, and other symptoms caused by a tropical parasite that he'd picked up in Asia along with both viral and bacterial infections.

Things were piling up: the burden of running the home, kids (did I mention there are four of them?), the stress of physical training, as well as the additional mental burden of caring for and worrying about my husband. Thus, I was not getting in the training that I wanted…needed…planned.

So before I knew it, there I was at a 10K race, the Neutraublinger Se(h)lauf, unsure of what to expect yet planning to use it as a test to see what I would be able to accomplish in the half marathon two weeks later. At the starting line I was dragged to the front of the pack by my other teammates (who are way faster than me), and you can't help but start off too fast or get steam-rolled. I ran the first 2 kilometers in 8 minutes and 20 seconds (6:40 min/ mile), and I knew I had to force myself to slow down because that was not a pace I could hold over 10 kilometers. But the damage was done, and although I finished in a respectable 46:43, I ran the race poorly. One highlight was getting passed by Sonja Tajsich (a world-class triathlete) at about kilometer 4 and her saying to me that it took her an awfully long time to catch up with me today. (Yes! But, obviously a fun-run for her since she can normally run a full marathon at that pace).

Needless to say, after my botched performance in the 10K, I wasn't very optimistic about my chances to meet my goal in the half marathon, namely, qualifying for the New York City Marathon, which, unlike Boston, allows qualification with either a half or full marathon.

In my daily training over the following two weeks, I incorporated a few speed sessions, alternating with mid- to long runs and throwing in a bit of strength training and drills, as well as some biking and yoga. I felt good. And then, upon seeing a hint of a glimmer on the horizon, I suddenly found myself several days before the race with extreme back pain and a skewed gait. An emergency adjustment from my physical therapist on my patio table the day before the half marathon put me back into alignment.

But, would it be enough?

It was.

The Regensburg Half Marathon is one of the highlights of my racing schedule every year since it is my hometown of choice— thousands of runners, many of whom I know or recognize from other events, friends cheering from along the course, and a city that I love. As usual, I ran with some friends, but this time my friend Matthias, who knew my time goal, encouraged me (and provided wind protection!) until I crossed the finish line.... in 1:41:17....good enough by 43 seconds for a New York City Marathon qualification!

I'd made it successfully through the first trimester!

SECOND TRIMESTER TRAINING

In August, eight months before the MdS, my training plan included a trail running camp in the Swiss Alps led by a man who'd run the MdS twice before—Timon Abegglen from Marmota Trailrunning. Three days of running—with full backpacks over 80-plus kilometers (50 miles), and 5,000 meters of positive elevation in an area encompassing the Greina Plateau—were planned.

Since I needed to be in Rabius-Surrein, Switzerland, at 11am on a Friday morning, and it was a whopping 440 kilometers (273 miles) from my home, I decided to drive to my friend Christina's in St. Gallen on Thursday and spend the night with her. Her daughter was there, too. Girl's night! Pajama party!

Then early the next morning I drove the remaining two hours, and, arriving about half an hour early, I easily found the small brick train station where a single person was waiting on a lonely bench outside. Of course, it was none other than Timon.

I stopped the car right in front of him and hopped out without even turning off the engine. I gave him a big hug (which kind of startled him), but I was so happy to finally meet him after emailing for weeks. A few minutes later our next compatriot was delivered by his wife, kids, and a monstrous dog. He greeted Timon, shook my hand, and introduced himself as Tom. Whew. I like easy names. Then a train screeched to a halt in front of us, and Timon announced that the next and final member of our small group had arrived. The only one departing the train was a mountain biker named Enrico, and our posse was complete. Timon explained that Enrico recently suffered a knee injury and instead of cancelling the weekend he decided to make the trek on bike.

A little small talk among the group (well, the small talk was among the guys, who were speaking Swiss, of which I understand almost nothing), and then we were off through the village for about a one-kilometer warm-up before the climb began. The incline did not start slowly, and the pace was not particularly tortoise either.

After about two kilometers I thought I was going to die.

Well, not die, but I knew my heart rate was very high, which was ridiculous after only ten minutes. Tom and Enrico were up ahead, but Timon was with me...obviously being the leader that was his job, otherwise I am sure he would have been off and away with the others.

Then a ray of hope appeared on my horizon of suffering. Timon said, "I've never had a group that has actually run through to this point. There have always been runners who have had to stop and walk before now." Hallelujah! That motivated me, and I powered on.

He said he uses the first few kilometers as a gauge to check the fitness level of the runners. I was relieved, but still in agony. Thankfully, shortly after that, the ascent became even steeper so Timon slowed to…a fast hiker's walk! Second that Hallelujah! I immediately followed suit while keeping Timon's pace, and my heart rate instantly slowed down. The trail remained steep and rough, and Enrico had to dismount the bike and walk. Things were improving by the minute! Ok, I know that's not very nice, but I didn't want to be the one to hold the group back.

We soon came to an alm—a mountain pasture—and took a few minutes' break to take photos, drink some water, and revel in the beauty of our surroundings.

The next several kilometers, though steadily uphill, were easy to traverse, and Timon entertained me with running lore.

By this time Enrico had ridden far ahead, and I was alone with Timon and Tom (T&T). Our next photo op was a hanging bridge over a gorge. (This is perhaps a good time to mention my fear of heights…what am I doing in the Alps then, you ask? Answer: Living life to the fullest. Like I tell my kids, "Have respect for everything. Don't be afraid of anything.") Tom took to running across the hanging bridge first with Timon shortly after him, which sent the sine waves out of control. So I waited until they were on the other side before scurrying across myself as fast as possible without looking down!

Back out onto the road we were soon surprised to find someone had made a small pile of rocks and laid a handful of wild raspberries on top! T&T laughed and ran by saying they were sure it was left there by Enrico (or Hansel and Gretel?), but I couldn't just run by and leave them there, so I scooped up the fruit and happily nibbled away.

I was also drinking a lot of water, and my 1.5 liters were empty fast, so I had to fill up a couple times in the river, which was pure enough to drink. Nothing like ice-cold Alpine water to quench your thirst! Then straight back to the trails. But the next time we had access to the river was when disaster struck.

Timon slipped while crossing some wet rocks. I saw him go down. I was actually pretty impressed with how he seemed to handle the impact, going right into a roll and then back up on his feet. But when he knelt down, began feeling his chin, and spitting out blood, I knew we had trouble.

Tom was over by the river's edge and hadn't seen what had happened. When I caught up to Timon and saw the blood, I kept trying to get Tom's attention, but it took a minute or two until he came over and realized something wasn't right. We examined Timon's chin and saw the damage. A deep cut about an inch long. Without question he would need stiches. He also had chipped a tooth and kept spitting out quite a lot of blood. Each of us had a variety of first aid supplies, and Tom and I taped up the wound as best as possible, but it wasn't holding well due to sweat and a day-old beard, so we bandaged his whole head to keep the tape in place.

Timon said we were only about a kilometer from the Hütte (Swiss chalet) where we were supposed to spend the night (though we later found out that we were still several kilometers away with some very difficult climbing), but we had no choice but to turn around and get him to a hospital. We also had no cell phone reception, so we couldn't contact Enrico. We decided the best thing to do was to give my car key to Tom, who would be the quickest down the mountain, while Timon and I would start to descend slowly and cross to the other side of the river and intersect with the dirt road where we could eventually meet up with Tom in the car.

Then the MdS lessons began.

Timon and I started to jog back down; he was injured but not one to complain, and he began talking about the Marathon des Sables that he had completed four months previously that April. He told me how he had had stomach problems and walked about 60 kilometers of the 90-kilometer fourth stage, but subsequently came back on the last day to finish tenth overall for that stage. Amazing.

We also talked about training. I mentioned how, in the upcoming months, I'd obviously be concentrating on endurance and leaving out the speed sessions altogether. He said, "No! You need to incorporate speed into your preparations!" Why? I asked. His answer was simple, not to mention sensible: "You need to get through each stage as quickly as possible, get out of the sun, get yourself under the tent, in the shade, and lie down with as much time to rest before you have to go out and do it again the next day." Obviously, he didn't mean sprint through the desert. The pace would still be slow, but just without wasting any time.

Timon then announced how his tongue was swelling up and getting numb, but that didn't stop him from talking, and the tips just kept coming. *You need to keep your sleeping bag in a plastic bag inside your backpack. Why? Because when you are so overheated and have some extra water, you want to dump it over your head; if the backpack and everything in it gets wet, you will have a very uncomfortable night in a damp sleeping bag when the temps drop to just above freezing.*

I couldn't believe everything I was hearing. Little things that I would never think of. *Crossing the sand dunes on the correct side where the wind sweeps across it since it's more compact and can carry your weight.*

How am I going to make it through this race? Then came my answer as Timon talked about his background in sports medicine and his work, not only as an organizer for running camps, but as a personal running coach. At first, he suggested that he would give me a credit for another trail running camp, since this one was obviously a wash, but I asked instead if he could apply it to coaching fees in preparation for the MdS. And the deal was done. That said, my training calendar was thankfully out of my hands and into that of an expert. No more worrying about trimesters, key races, or whether I was getting the right balance of long runs, tempo runs, and hill work. I was now in good hands.

We were still high up on the mountain, though, and Timon's head was pounding. Eventually I saw my black SUV snaking up the windy, narrow road. *Relief.*

We finally got Timon to a hospital, where we stayed with him until he was released with five stitches, and then loaded him onto the next train back to Zurich. And, yes, he finally was able to get in touch with Enrico who was at the Hütte and wondering what had happened to us!

It was getting late. I was four hours from home, exhausted, and had nowhere to sleep. Tom was still there, and he offered a simple solution. He and his wife (and three kids and two dogs) had a small apartment not far away, and I could spend the night there if I didn't mind sleeping on the couch. He called his wife, she said no problem, and she was even willing to cook a vegan dinner for me!

Tom's family was great, and the dogs were immediately my best friends (hoped they did not sleep in the living room, though). During dinner, Tom and I planned to go back the next day to where we left off and make it up to Greina Hochebene for a half-day run, and then I would head home. But the evening wasn't over until the kids and I had played croquet into the night.

Needless to say, the weekend turned out to be a great time, and Tom and I decided to stay in touch. The next time we saw each other was several months later in October, again in Switzerland, where we both took part in the back-to-back races of the Transruinaulta (42.2 kilometers, 1800 meters elevation) on Saturday and the Transviamala (19 kilometers, 850 meters elevation) on Sunday. This was a great mental siege for me since it was my first back-to-back race and, in a few months, I'd have to run six marathons in a week across the Sahara Desert.

The following months over the winter were the culmination of my training, and under Timon's expert guidance, I knew I was on the right track. Workouts included strength training three times per week that didn't use weights but rather my own bodyweight: push-ups, sit-ups, planks, squats, lunges, and so on. The indoor bike also made an appearance three times per week, often in combination with running (i.e., a 90-minute run then 90 minutes on the bike). Bags of flour, sugar, and coffee beans were packed tightly into my backpack that I was now carrying twice a week on distances up to 20 kilometers. This began with 3 kilograms and was eventually increased up to 6. This is a critical part of training as a weighted pack is not only strenuous, but it also alters gait and should be gotten used to. (But my shoulders would still be in agony after running through the desert with a week full of supplies on my back!) And, of course, I was steadily increasing my distances, running over 100 kilometers per week in the final six weeks until I peaked at 132 kilometers prior to tapering for two weeks before the race.

Physically, I was in excellent condition, the best of my life. Coach said I was trained to a professional level. But as everyone knows, when it comes to finishing ultras, physical preparedness is irrelevant if you are not mentally strong. I was nervous and a little scared. So, even though my body was ready, would I be mentally tough enough for this challenge?

CHAPTER 6

RIDING WITH A WORLD CHAMPION

Before we get back into the desert, let's finish this topic of training.

Biking is a really important type of physical exercise because it can very effectively help increase endurance when used in combination with running, and it gives the joints a break from pounding the pavement.

During my preparation for the MdS, I went for a bike ride with Bernhard Steinberger, a world champion of ultradistance cycling, who I'd met about a year before when he joined up with the Armin Wolf Running Team to race with us at the 24-hour bike race in Kelheim, which he'd won previously as a soloist.

Ultradistance cycling world champion Bernhard Steinberger

© Bernhard Steinberger

What the heck is ultradistance cycling, you ask? Think long… very long…like, we are not talking hours, rather days, on a bike. Without stopping…okay, a few minutes here and there for the most basic of necessities, but that's it.

These are examples of what it takes to be an ultracyclist: The Glocknerman is an ultracycling marathon of 1,025 kilometers (637 miles) and 15,743 meters (more than 51,000 feet) elevation through the Austrian Alps. Bernhard came in third overall and first in his age group at the Glocknerman in 2008 and 2014, thus winning the world championship titles for his class; he finished in 40 hours in 2014. Race Around Ireland (RAI) covers a distance of 2,209 kilometers (1,373 miles) with 24,083 meters (almost 80,000 feet) elevation, and in 2013 he had a second-place finish in 116 hours (yes, that's 4 days and 20 hours!), but in 2015 he won the race outright! And the list goes on and on.

THE ARMIN WOLF LAUFTEAM (RUNNING TEAM)

The Armin Wolf Running Team, based in Regensburg, Germany, is a non-profit group of athletes who participate in sporting events with a charitable focus. A sponsorship pool provides donations, which are distributed to various local private or public organizations in need.

The team was founded in 2010 by sports journalist Armin Wolf and his wife Alexandra, who organize the donations, races, and other events. In addition to running for a good cause, the athletes also visit schools to motivate children to participate in sports and live healthy lifestyles.

He's a good runner, too, which you'd never really guess when you meet the guy. He is my height at best, and his quads are as thick as tree trunks. But somehow, perhaps generations ago, deep in the Bavarian hills, a genetic combination was created which gave him an incredible gift for both speed and endurance. *Voilà!*

I contacted Bernhard and asked him if he'd go for a training ride with me up in the area where he lives. He immediately said yes and asked about how long I would like to ride and whether I'd prefer the terrain flat, hilly, or mountainous. I replied hilly to mountainous (when in Rome!) and that about 2.5 to 3 hours would probably be about my limit with him. A day later he replied that he'd selected a route that should take us about four hours and has one really big mountain in it. *Ugh.* Then the next day he texted me and asked about my bike gears, concerned if I'd be able to handle the mountainous 10% grades. *What have I gotten myself into?*

Bernhard with quads as thick as tree trunks

© Bernhard Steinberger

And to top it off, the weather that day called for cool temps and heavy rain. Perfect training weather for Bernhard's next *Race Around Ireland*, but all I could envision was descending that mountain on dangerously slippery roads!

It was evident from the start who the novice was and who the pro was. He evaluated my gear: You have a helmet? *Check.* You'll

67

be too cold in shorts. *Check. Change clothes.* Here's a windproof vest to wear on top. *Check. Thanks.* You don't have shoe covers? *Uh, no.* At which point he disappeared into his house for a few minutes and came back with a pair for me. *Check.* What do you have to drink? *Water.* Just water? *Yes.* Again, he disappeared and came back a minute later with two packets of PowerGels which he squeezed into my water bottle and shook with a vengeance. *I thought I had things covered. This is getting embarrassing.*

As we got started, it was immediately clear that he was a really good riding partner, timely letting me know where the turns were and what was to come. After about an hour riding, and still several kilometers before the mega-mountain, he told me that if I needed to eat something this would be a good time prior to the climb, so I ate half a banana and washed it down with "powered-up" water. I asked him whether he was going to eat anything. His answer, "Don't take this the wrong way…but the pace is not really high. I'm not burning many calories." *Sigh.* Everything is relative.

Chillin' with a beer and Bernhard after one of our team running events

He did most of the talking in response to my questions about his athletic history, injuries, races, and biking technique. His answers were refreshing…nothing "textbook" about them. Bernhard is essentially a self-taught rider and bikes because he loves it. It is his passion. Which is exactly what he calls himself: *"Sportler aus Leidenschaft."* *A Passionate Athlete.* And it's not only the biking he loves. At one point, when the view opened up for miles, he gestured with a proud smile to the rolling farmlands interspersed with clusters of pine forests and said, "This is home."

We got lucky with the weather, as it stayed mostly overcast though cool, and we only had about 10 minutes of rain in a tour that took us about 3 hours 15 minutes to finish. That was plenty for me, but not for Bernhard. He was going inside for a quick change of clothes and then meeting another friend for a few more hours on the bike. And after that he'd go on a short one-hour run before calling it a day. Sounds like a lot, but I guess that's what one should expect from a world champion.

So, now that we're well trained, it's time to get back to the desert.

CHAPTER 7

MDS DAY 2: LOGISTICS

SATURDAY, APRIL 9, LOGISTICS CHECK-IN AT BIVOUAC 1

6:00.   Woke up after a terrible night's sleep on the bare ground with only a thin carpet under me. It had become very cold during the night, and I had put on my light fleece jacket, but despite wearing all of the warm clothing I had and being tucked deep inside my sleeping bag which was supposed to keep me warm at temperatures as low as 8 °C (46 °F), I still shivered.

8:00.   Breakfast in the bivouac: flatbread, water, orange juice, coffee. No eggs for me.

10:00.   All of us returned to our tents to make last-minute decisions about what to keep in the backpack and what to give up at the logistic checks when we turned in our suitcases. The most significant decision I made was to

Bivouac at the Marathon des Sables
© MARATHON DES SABLES 2016

keep the fleece jacket. Actually, it was not even fleece, just a very lightweight mixed fabric with a hood, but it was a critical decision for which I was so thankful later during those cold nights!

Suddenly, there was an acidic smell wafting through our tent. I knew it from somewhere but couldn't place it at first in the foreign surroundings. Then I turned around to see Beatrice with a bottle of nail polish in one hand, daintily painting her toenails with the other. I gave her my best "you have got to be kidding me" look, and she explained how it was the last chance for a week, and she promised me she would pack the nail polish in her suitcase and not carry it with her through the desert. I had my doubts.

12:00.   Lunch in the bivouac: Rice. Grilled veggies. Keep drinking that water.

14:00. Last chance for checking and packing the backpack before we said goodbye to everything else that went into our suitcases, which were handed over to the organization. We would get our luggage back when arriving at our hotel in Ouarzazate after the last day of the race—a week later!

There was a minimum weight requirement of 6.5 kilograms (14 pounds) for the backpack to ensure everyone was carrying enough provisions. Our tentmate Mike had a scale and weighed our bags in the tent before we had to go to the official logistical check-in. My backpack weighed 7 kilograms (15 pounds). More than I thought. At home it was 6.3 without the marathon kit, and I'd added a few things, so I was expecting about 6.8 kilograms. Now, with the marathon kit, which I would be receiving shortly from the staff, it would be about 7.5 kilograms. But it was still lighter than everyone's except for Mike who'd run the race before and had scaled back on everything. He even had to add a couple of oranges to his pack to get it over 6,500 grams.

15:00. I was surprised when I got to the check-in station and hung my backpack on the scale…it first read 5.8 kilograms! That couldn't be possible! I fiddled with the scale to bring it into balance, and the needle shot up to 7 kilograms. Obviously the scale was not very accurate, but my pack was thankfully over the minimum level.

17:00. Back at the tent I decided to write down my experiences so far, and when I pulled out my diary, I got shocked looks from the others in the tent because I had such a "large" notebook with me, especially since they all knew how obsessed I was with cutting back on weight! But the book only weighed 100 grams. I'd gotten it in Nepal, and it was made of lightweight recycled paper. For me it was well worth it to have it along so that I could write all my memories down each day while they were still fresh in my mind.

My lightweight MdS diary

19:00. Dinner—last large hot meal for the next week! Couscous with cinnamon and raisins. Cooked carrots and zucchini. Moroccan bread, large round loaves cut in quarters. They also had cans of Coke for us, but I took it with me to drink in the morning as I didn't want the caffeine keeping me up at night. And although we were sitting on the ground, the luxury of eating off the low table was something to be missed in the coming days.

20:00. In bed and trying desperately to sleep despite the anxiety and anticipation of the upcoming challenge!

A few hours earlier I'd given away my suitcase with all my comforts and was left with only a backpack for the next seven days. Though I checked and cross-checked my list a million times, I could only hope I had everything that I would need to get me across 257 kilometers (160 miles) of the Moroccan Sahara.

CHAPTER 8

MY MDS PACK LIST

The minimum weight requirement of the backpack according to the regulations of the MdS was, ironically enough, the same that Coach Timon had given me. I say ironically because he gave me the value as a weight *limit*, a maximum, not a minimum value. Without the marathon kit, which is supplied by the race organizers at check-in, he said my pack should not weigh more than 6.5 kilograms (14 pounds). High standards, Coach!

This is an unbelievable target when you consider what needs to be included in that pack: sleeping bag, clothing, headlamp, camera, personal and safety items, oh, and food. For a week. Essentially everything that I will require to survive seven days in the Sahara Desert needs to be carried on my back, except for water.

You have to weigh the pros and cons. Do I really need that extra pair of shorts? A pillow? Mattress? And how many calories are essential to get me through the rigors of each day? Can I live on dried fruit, nuts, and granola bars? Or will I crave a hot meal after trekking for endless hours across the dunes under a scorching sun?

My coach said, "You either NEED an item, or you DON'T. There is no middle ground. If you think you MAY use something, or it MIGHT BE NICE TO HAVE...then leave it at home." Consider this, if my backpack at the start, with marathon kit, weighs 7 kilograms (15 pounds) and my bodyweight is 54 kilograms (119 pounds), then I am lugging 13% of my bodyweight in an environment that is already forcing my pulse to rise and my body temperature to increase...even when I am sitting in the shade.

Analyzing my options

For months I spent endless hours analyzing food calorie content versus weight, scouring the Internet for the lightest safety items on the market, and testing whether my stomach could handle certain high-calorie-dense, low-weight foods.

Then, in late February, six weeks before I headed to Morocco, I packed all my gear together and headed south across the border into Switzerland where I met with Coach Timon to go through my pack list, item by item.

And here's where we landed...

First, the Essentials, consisting of the mandatory equipment required by the rules and also the marathon kit provided upon check-in, all of which needed to be carried at all times or penalties could be incurred. (All weights are shown in grams, whereby 100 grams are equal to about 3.5 ounces, and 1000 grams are 2.2 pounds.)

Mandatory Equipment	Description	Weight (g)
Backpack w/ bottles, whistle	WAA MdS rucksack with one side pocket	900
Sleeping bag	Sea to Summit, Spark SPI	400
Head torch w/ spare batteries	Black Diamond (62+ 36 + 36)	134
10 safety pins		3
Compass	Recta DT200	29
Lighter		15
Knife with metal blade	X-ACTO knife	10
Topical disinfectant	Sterilium, 100 ml	107
Anti-venom pump	VeniStop	37
Signaling mirror	*Initially 20 g, then cut it down to 13*	13
Aluminum survival sheet	Tatonka 210 x 160 cm	64
Sun screen	La Roche-Posay, 50+	62
Cash	200 Euro	4
Total		**1785**
Marathon Kit		
Road book		80
SPOT Gen3	Satellite tracker/time measurement	124
Salt tablets		50
Toilet sachets		150
ID marks	Punch cards	20
Total		**424**

I chose the MdS backpack from WAA because it has everything that you need for this race, and it better had, because that's what it was specifically designed for. (Check out my YouTube channel for tips on use and customization of the backpack.) I looked at a few other bags from Salomon and Raidlight, but the fit and functionality were not optimal for me and this race.

Marathon des Sables backpack developed by WAA

The Sea to Summit Spark SPI sleeping bag was chosen simply on the recommendation of my coach. It's light, compact, he used it in the desert, it worked. Period. But it's wasn't cheap.

I bought the Black Diamond headlamp two years ago for a 24-hour bike race, and although it's not the lightest on the market, it's a good quality one, and I couldn't justify coughing up a ton of money for a new one which I'd never need again just to save a few grams.

Timon took one look at my compass and said it was too big and that I should cut the flange off. Had to search for that Japanese precision saw I've got hidden in the garage.

My little metal-bladed X-ACTO knife usually finds its home in my office, and I use it to open packages. Opening a box with it one day I realized that it is probably about the lightest knife I'm going to find, and it would be perfect for the MdS. Turns out I wasn't the only one with this bright idea. Beatrice had one, and Timon had also used the same when he was in the desert.

Mandatory equipment for the MdS

The signaling mirror also got a nix from Timon, and he said if I couldn't find a smaller and lighter one, then the Japanese saw would have double duty. Check.

The weight of the items in the Marathon Kit were a guesstimate, but I had no control over it anyway. It's all gotta be schlepped!

Next up…clothing! No, it's not required, but definitely essential.

Clothing Item	Description	Weight (g)
Sahara hat	Salomon	58
Short-sleeve top	Raidlight	99
Shorts	Loose-fitting with built in slip	83
Calf sleeves	Skins	53
Sunglasses	Nike Impel Swift	23
Buff	Buff	32
Running shoes/ gaiters	Inov-8 X-Talon 212/WAA Gaiters	650
Sports bra	Patagonia	26
Socks	Injinii toe socks	34
Total on body		**1058**
Sand-proof glasses	WAA-MdS	51
Compression tights for recovery	XBionic, long	160
Underwear	Patagonia	19
Shirt	True Religion lightweight T-shirt Review Light shirt 70g	70
Extra socks	Falke RU4W	31
Windbreaker	Salomon Fast Wing Hoodie	70
Slippers	Renaissance Hotel Hamburg	58
Total in backpack		**459**

The Sahara hat from Salomon had a hole in the back for my ponytail! Reason enough to choose it. The neck flap was detachable, and believe it or not, I never used it. You cover every inch of exposed flesh with the highest SPF sun screen anyway and having my neck exposed allowed cooling from any slight gust of wind, which was always welcome.

I selected a short-sleeve top from Raidlight because it is very light and breathable. It has a half-zip in the front so I could adjust it for cooling; it covered up my neck so the backpack straps wouldn't have contact with my skin; it has gel application spots on the shoulders to reduce slippage of the backpack; and it has side pockets for granola bars, salt tablets, nuts, iso tabs…whatever. When I got to the MdS, I was surprised to see that Elisabeth Barnes, who had won the race the previous year, had the same shirt! It must be good!

Note on material: Please make sure you train with the shirt you are planning on wearing at the MdS (or any other long-distance event with a backpack), even with other layers on top and then your backpack, to see how your skin reacts to the material under the weight of your pack. Many people swear by Merino wool, but I have mixed feelings about it. I think it is a great material when you require a bit of extra warmth as a first layer when doing outdoor winter activities that do not require significant sweating, such as hiking, skiing, and biking. But when I run in Merino wool, my sweat is simply stored in the shirt and comes off in a soggy mess when I'm done; although, I have to admit, wet or not, it does keep you warm. Another huge negative is that when worn under a backpack it rubs against the skin and causes chafing. I looked like I had a bad sunburn when I was testing out a Merino wool shirt under my backpack. This may not be the case for everyone, but I've heard the same from others, so try it yourself to be sure!

Originally, I wanted to wear loose shorts with a built-in slip, but they were very short, and I was afraid that if my legs swelled slightly then the thighs could rub against each other and each step could become agony. So I changed my mind to the compression shorts from Skins (in pink) which are very comfortable and light. When I showed them to Timon, he laughed and said he was familiar with the Skins products and that if I don't rinse them out daily they'll be standing on their own after a couple of days, but I was planning on doing a bit of "laundry" each day anyway. Then, for some reason, I just couldn't get used to the Skins. They were too low in the back, and the thought of wearing something tight in the desert was not appealing. And whether it was also Coach's comments or the thought of not trusting my favorite shorts, at the last minute, I switched back to my original plan of the loose shorts and was glad I did.

I chose the calf sleeves from Skins simply because I find them more comfortable than those from other makers. I don't like to run in them but use them for recovery. I wasn't sure beforehand for which function (or both) I'd be using them in Morocco, but I wanted to have them along.

My tried-and-true Nike Impel Swift sunglasses have never let me down, so they got to come along with me, although they were trashed by the wind-whipped sand by the time I was through.

The Inov-8 X-Talon 212s were my shoe of choice. I also considered something from Salomon, but on the advice of my coach (who also wore these) and from my own experience with the shoe, I decided to go with Inov-8s. They are very minimalist and not at all good for roads, but on the trails they are really like a second skin...light, breathable, and plenty of space in the toe box. Plus, in the desert, you don't need much cushioning as the terrain is relatively soft.

I bought the WAA-MdS gaiters and had the Velcro application stitched into the upper part of the shoes by Timon's trusted Italian cobbler in Zurich. How can you go wrong with that? Note on the zipper for the gaiters: After a day in the desert, the zipper gets filled with tiny sand fragments and gets jammed, so if you can't unzip them at the end of the day, then just pour a little water over the zipper, and it will free it up immediately.

My itsy-bitsy Patagonia sports bra weighs only 26 grams. Of all the nights I've cried over not being blessed with a hefty front rack, I can honestly say I can't imagine running with much more than those little size As. P.S. Thanks, God!

Injinii toe socks! Separate the toes and you separate the sand that happens to get into your shoes and thus avoid chafing. I carried an extra pair of regular socks in the pack…just in case I couldn't get my toes into the toe sockets for some ungodly reason which I hoped never to encounter.

There is not a huge market for sand-proof goggles, so I had to go with the ones from WAA although they are slightly too big for my face. Timon says if worse comes to worst and there is a bad sandstorm, then I can cut two small eye holes in my buff and wrap it up and over my glasses. Good to know, but I was hoping that would remain just a useful mental note. Quite honestly, even though we experienced a pretty nasty sandstorm on the first day, I never used the sand-proof goggles; my sunglasses were adequate.

My camp clothes consisted of long compression tights from XBionic, a lightweight T-shirt, and slippers nipped from the Renaissance Hotel in Hamburg. I also had the Fast Wing Hoodie from Salomon for wind protection. Although it provides no warmth and breathability is minimal if at all, it is my absolute favorite piece of running clothing that I own.

Now comes my own material which I chose to bring, necessary in my own eyes, but not required. This list will naturally vary wildly among runners.

Own Material	Description	Weight (g)
Camera	Lenco HD400; water- and sand-proof	121
Watch	Polar, no GPS	42
Plastic spoon		3
Diary		108
Pencil		2
Ziplock plastic bags for clothes, road book, sleeping bag, daily food, sanitary items		50
Toothbrush, -paste		11
Soap, small bar		10
Toilet paper/wipes		30
Mini compressed towels	10 pieces	28
Blistex		10
Ear plugs		7
Total		**422**

My husband gave me a Go-Pro knock-off camera for Christmas, but unfortunately I left it turned on during the first night there and the battery ran down, so I had to carry it with me for the week or throw it out. I carried it.

I decided not to bring my GPS Garmin watch since I didn't want to worry about having to charge it and lug a solar charger. I'd need a watch to keep a basic check on my pace and how often I was drinking, so I brought my simple Polar watch without GPS.

The plastic spoon I chose was the lightest I could find. It was from one of the doll house sets from my daughters. This was a poor choice in the end since it reacted with the heat of the food and began to deteriorate.

The only real "luxury" item I brought was a small book to be used as a diary so I could write down my daily adventures and make sketches when they were fresh in my head. You are reaping the benefits of this decision now as you are reading this book.

Personal hygiene articles were, of course, to include a small travel plastic toothbrush and toothpaste, a small bar of soap, and well, toilet paper is also BYO. In addition, I dried out some personal hygiene wipes and could simply add a bit of water to get an extra good cleaning. Hoped my fellow runners, at least my tentmates, would do the same.

I also decided to take some compressed mini towels. They are dried and compressed to the size of a bon-bon, and when you add a tiny bit of water to them they begin to release, and you can unroll them and open them up to a size a bit larger than a Kleenex, but of a relatively robust gauzy-towelish material. I planned to use them with a bit of soap for washing my face, feet, and so forth, and then I could simply throw the dirty ones away. These turned out to be a fabulous luxury item.

A tube of Blistex is a MUST for sun protection of my lips, as well as ear plugs to help me get a good night's sleep. (Yeah, wishful thinking, right?)

And…last but not least, what you've all been waiting for…FOOD!

Food Item/Day	Amount (unit or grams)	Calories/ 100g	Calories/ unit	Total Calories	Weight/ unit	Total Weight
Two of the short days and rest day (3 days)						
BP-WR	2	486	270	540	56	112
Nutrixxion	1	398	219	219	55	55
Millenium	1	476	400	400	84	84
Cashews/Almonds	50	553	NA	276	NA	50
Dried mango	50	319	319	159	50	50
Dehydrated meal	191	350	350	668	191	191
Sponsor EAC	10	NA	4.9	49	1.4	14
Isotonic Nuun tabs	2	NA	16	32	5	10
Dried coffee	1	NA	0	0	2	2
Subtotal				**2343**		**568**
Subtotal 3 days				**7029**		**1704**
Two short days						
BP-WR	2	486	270	540	56	112
Nutrixxion	1	398	219	219	55	55
Millenium	2	476	400	800	84	168
Cashews/Almonds	50	553	NA	276	NA	50
Dried mango	50	319	319	159	50	50
Sponsor EAC	10	NA	4.9	49	1.4	14
Isotonic Nuun tabs tttttabstabs	2	NA	16	32	5	10
Dried coffee	1	NA	0	0	2	2
Subtotal				**2075**		**461**
Subtotal 2 days				**4150**		**922**
Long day						
BP-WR	2		270	540	56	112
Nutrixxion	1		219	219	55	55
Millenium	3		400	1200	84	252
Cashews/Almonds	50		553	276	NA	50
Dried mango	50		319	159	50	50

(continued)

Food Item/Day	Amount (unit or grams)	Calories/ 100g	Calories/ unit	Total Calories	Weight/ unit	Total Weight
Sponsor EAC	10		4.9	49	1.4	14
Isotonic Nuun tabs	2		16	32	5	10
Dried coffee	1		0	0	2	2
Subtotal				2475		545
BP-WR	2		270	540	56	112
Charity stage						
Millenium	2		400	800	84	168
Cashews/Almonds	50		553	276	NA	50
Dried mango	50		319	159	50	50
Dried coffee	1		0	0	2	2
Subtotal				1775		382
Weekly Total				15429		3553

I was not 100% convinced of this nutritional strategy beforehand, primarily based on sports bars and nuts, but in the end, it worked out perfectly.

My breakfast each day consisted of two BP-WR bars and freeze-dried coffee for my needed caffeine kick. Since I wasn't planning on bringing a stove or a cooking pot, the coffee would be drunk cold. The BP-WR bars are highly condensed wheat biscuits with a high energy density of 270 calories per 55-gram bar, so I'd already be getting over 500 calories in for breakfast. They are often used in emergency situations like war, floods, or anywhere there is a supply crisis. With a balanced range of vitamins, carbohydrates, proteins, fats, and dietary fiber, they are crucial for survival when food supplies are lacking...or when running 257 kilometers through the Sahara desert...similar situation.

On the run I'd be eating Nutrixxion and Millenium bars, which are also similar to the BPs in calorie density and nutritional value, but have different flavors to keep me entertained, namely, cappuccino, cherry, and raspberry. At home I roast my own cashews and almonds and add soy sauce to them. Since I don't eat meat, nuts are a great source of protein, not to mention salt, which would be critical during this race. I'd also be taking some dried mango just 'cause I love it, and I thought I may want a sour-flavor kick.

Precise measurement of my food rations

I took three Trek 'n Eat dehydrated meals with me, not necessarily for the calorie content, since they are considerably less calorie dense than my sports bars, but because I was afraid that I would crave a hot meal in the evenings which the bars and nuts couldn't satisfy. Again, since I didn't have a stove, I planned to just put water directly into the meal bag and let it sit in the sun for an hour in the hot sand to boil. These meals were intended for the two short days (single marathon) and the rest day, but on the long day (double marathon), I was definitely not planning on eating one of these since once I was finally back at camp after 15 or more hours, I was sure that all I'd want to do is crawl into my sleeping bag and not have the energy capable to cook or to eat such a huge quantity of food.

To top off the nutritional requirements, I'd be taking Sponser Pro Amino EAC tablets which contain an amino acid complex to help speed up regeneration. I also had NUUN tabs to pop into a couple water bottles per day for an isotonic drink that would replenish some of the sodium, potassium, magnesium, and calcium that I'd lose through sweat.

As a last-minute thought, I threw in a small bag of chia seeds. If they work for the Tarahumara, they should work for me.

And that's it! So, what's the final tally?

Total weight—Food	3553 g	7.82 lbs
Total weight—Own material	422 g	0.93 lbs
Total weight—Mandatory	2209 g	4.86 lbs
Weight of clothing in pack	459 g	1.01 lbs
Total weight of backpack	**6643 g**	**14.62 lbs**

I was ready as I was ever going to be, so let's get this show on the road!

All my food rations for 7 days in the Sahara desert

CHAPTER 9

MDS STAGE 1

OUEST ERG CHEBBI TO ERG ZNAIGUI, 34 KM

The sand dunes were daunting. They dominated the view from bivouac1. From the Road Book we all knew that the first day would entail getting across those massive mounds of beautifully-sculptured sand, but what we didn't know was that Mother Nature had something else in store for us that day which would make crossing the miles of dunes feel like a walk in the park.

5:30. The camp began to stir, and despite having earplugs in, I was awake, too. I hid inside the warmth and safety of my sleeping bag for another half an hour before stretching my upper body out of the sleeping bag to look for my breakfast.

6:00. Breakfast that morning, as every day that week, consisted of two BP-WR bars and cold instant coffee. The bars are actually quite good and taste like English biscuits. The only drawback with them is that they are very, very dry and crumbly, which is why I was having them for breakfast rather than on the run. I could eat them carefully while sitting in the tent and make sure I didn't lose too many precious calories as crumbs on the ground.

7:00. I began getting my backpack ready for the day, putting all the food that I would require while running in the small front pack. While still half in the sleeping bag, I got dressed into my race clothes. Then I reluctantly crawled out of the warmth and safety of my sleeping bag. It was very cold. I had my light fleece jacket plus my windbreaker on over my running shirt. I rolled up and stuffed the sleeping bag into a tiny little storage bag, and subsequently into a second waterproof plastic bag.

7:30. Collect water rations. Fill water bottles. Complete final packing.

8:00. Use the toilets, the event of which I refer to as the "walk of shame." It was actually a pretty clever solution of bringing Western toilets into the desert, but the degree of privacy for accomplishing this most basic of bodily functions was at a minimum. There were three toilets in a group, each surrounded by heavy tarps as "curtains." The toilet itself was like a plastic folding stool, but with a hole in the middle. We were given toilet sachets (plastic bags) which were to be secured around the top of the stool, with the bag hanging down through the middle. We were told to find a small rock on the way to the loo and then drop the rock into the bag to open it up and weigh it down. So we were actually able to sit down on a clean surface—the plastic bag covering the rim of the stool—inside a closed stall. But, your neighbor was just a foot or so on the other side of the curtain, all noises were detectable for everyone around, the curtains were not able to be secured well, so anytime the wind blew, which was often, the curtains blew around and everyone standing and waiting in line got a glimpse of you with your shorts around your ankles, but you couldn't hold the curtain shut because you are busy holding that one corner of the plastic bag that doesn't stay stretched around the stool, and the bags are too small anyway, and if the bag becomes too heavy it will slip down and through to the ground where all of its contents will spill out. So forget about urinating in the bag, that had to be done before you even lined up behind four or five others, with heads tucked down in shame, in front of one of those three cubicles, watching as those who'd finished came out with a small brown plastic bag,

Beatrice and the toilets

tied at the top with a knot, and tossed it into the waiting large plastic garbage can.

With the deed done, I headed back to where our tent had once been but was now being rapidly rounded-up by the local helpers. We sat on the rolled-up rugs, waiting for the word that things were about to start. The suspense was killing us.

8:15. All of the runners were asked to assemble into the form of a giant number 31, as that year marked the 31st anniversary of the running of the MdS, so they could take photos from the helicopter. Police tape had been set up in the form of the numbers, and we just had to find a spot while the helicopter swooped down low over our heads.

8:45. Headed to the starting line.

9:00. At the starting line, the tension in the air was palpable as we all knew what lay just ahead. Patrick Bauer, the race organizer and founder, stood on top of an SUV with his translator and gave us the daily news and race instructions. Checkpoints and water rations were relayed. Birthdays were announced, and we sang "Happy Birthday." Then the song that we all knew was coming, the song which would send us off every day into the desert, began to be heard softly and grew progressively louder until the refrain was blaring, runners were dancing, and all were howling out the lyrics… we were most definitively setting out on *A Highway to Hell*. Before we knew it, the countdown was on, the helicopter was swooping in on us, and finally we were in motion.

The 31st Marathon des Sables in the Moroccan Sahara Desert was underway.

Start of the 31st Marathon des Sables

The helicopter flew to the front of the pack and subsequently turned and sideswiped the entire queue of runners not 10 meters (30 feet) over our heads. The roar of the engines was deafening. The adrenaline was on full tilt, and my legs and body felt strong after two weeks of tapering.

The race started out with three kilometers of flat ground interspersed with sandy areas where running was comfortably easy. Daredevil helicopter maneuvers followed us throughout this entire section. Such stunts would never be allowed in the "civilized world." It was scary but exciting.

Entering the dunes so early in the race meant that the runners were still densely packed, and everyone tried their best to run when the terrain was flat or downhill, but then amicably queued when there was a dune to climb or a ridge to follow.

The dunes of Erg Chebbi near Merzouga are massive seas of ridges formed by wind-blown sand that lie adjacent to the Algerian border. The dunes are 150 meters (490 feet) high in places and span an area of about 50 kilometers (30 miles) north to south and up to 10 kilometers (6 miles) across. A more beautiful work of nature would be difficult to find, and despite the strenuous work entailed in crossing them, their magnificence could not be overlooked. At one point, while traversing a ridge that fell off dramatically to my right and left, I couldn't help but be awestruck by the perfect pinnacle of the crest of the dune and how it gently curved and fell off to its own liking.

Sand dunes: beautiful forms of nature
© Gabriel Biguria

It is nearly impossible to run in the dunes, except downhill, but even that takes some skill and coordination, which I did not have, because the sand is so fine it simply absorbs the momentum of each step, requiring much more energy than covering the same distance on a packed surface. Anyone who has gone running on the beach or schlepped their gear through the deep sand while trying to find

Miles of dunes to traverse
© MARATHON DES SABLES 2016

Running through the sand amid mounds of camel grass
© MARATHON DES SABLES 2016

that perfect spot at the shorefront, knows exactly what I am talking about. We crossed 12 kilometers (7 miles) of the sandy dunes, which took me just over two hours. I breathed a sigh of relief thinking that the "worst" of the day was over, but I was soon to find out that the battle was just about to begin.

11:15. Checkpoint 1 at kilometer 15. Filled water bottles and ate half of a sports bar. Just after leaving the checkpoint, a headwind kicked up, which initially brought cool relief, and although the terrain was now flat, the going was still slowed by sand and rocks. We ran across expanse fields strewn with sharp-edged pieces of coal as far as the eye could see, tossed across the landscape in jagged chunks of all sizes ranging from matchbox cars to encyclopedias, so dense you couldn't avoid the smaller ones with each step. Concentration was required, as a misstep could cause a fall, and the sharp edges of the coal could certainly cause a nasty injury. I was mostly able to stay on track by keeping an eye on the runners ahead of me, although the course was marked every few hundred meters with spray paint on stones or pieces of fabric tied to a post or a bush. Only occasionally was there actually a trail or dirt road to follow, so we were left on our own to determine the best path to traverse between the course markings. Sometimes the shortest route was not the easiest nor the fastest, such as in the canyons or in the dunes, but after a couple of days of self-taught desert navigation, it got easier to read the terrain.

13:00. Checkpoint 2 at kilometer 25.8. The wind never relented, but began to grow stronger. We were in the middle of a sandstorm. The ferocious winds kicked up the sand, whirling and twirling it around us, piercing it against my skin. I had to keep my head down to keep the sand out of my eyes and to be safe on every step. Visibility was restricted but still good enough to keep moving on. But then I looked up in the distance to see yet another mass of thick sand being blown to and fro with an unpredictable path like that of a tornado. I couldn't tell exactly which direction it was moving, and it was often changing course.

I could only hope and pray that it would blow itself away from me, but closer and closer it inevitably came until there was nowhere else to go to avoid it. Suddenly it was right before my eyes, and I turned my head away and tightened my body to brace for the impact. It stopped me in my tracks and was painful as the sand spat against my bare skin. I was temporarily blinded but also lucky that the high-density area was small and soon I could see well enough again to keep moving, just to get the stage over with and back to the relative safety of the camp and my tent.

At one point I was stopped by photographers who were shocked to see my face completely blackened by the sooty soil which had been dredged up by the wind and redeposited on my skin, no doubt held in place by the sunscreen heavily applied that morning.

14:51. Five hours and fifty-one minutes after I'd started I finally crossed the finish line, the first of six that week, and placed 22nd among the women that day out of more than 200 (over 1,100 runners in all). Not bad for starters.

I drank a small cup of mint tea, offered to all runners at the finish, but it was not at all refreshing; it was hot, too hot, though I drank it because the sugar would do me good. Then I collected my three bottles of water (1.5 liters each) and trudged off to my tent where I found that I was the first one there, which meant "tent duty:" lifting the rug and clearing the underlying ground of stones. But first things first. Remove the backpack, collapse onto the carpet, and lie immobile for an indeterminable amount of time.

My shoulders were in agony, the muscles connecting the shoulder to the neck was where I carried all the weight of the backpack. I could not lift my arms without being in excruciating pain. How was I going to carry the pack again tomorrow? The rest of the week?

Drink and eat. I knew this was necessary, but it had to be forced. I ate some of the cashews that I'd brought and had roasted in soy sauce at home. A great source of protein and salt (best snack for athletes; see my recipe in the appendix). They were exactly what I needed and not too heavy, as my appetite was minimal anyway. Next up was tent duty. I folded up the rug on either side and used my feet to scrape away the stones and even out the soil. Mike returned after about an hour and helped me finish the job. He'd run the MdS a few times before and was the veteran of our group; we were constantly going to him with questions and asking for advice. He showed me how to take one of the larger sticks used to hold up the tent (there were always one or two extra at each tent) and sweep it across the ground to loosen up the embedded rocks. It was quickly done with his help and then we could spread out our things and relax, well, maybe recover would be a better word. But before I could do that, there was one more thing that desperately needed taking care of. With the help of some water I rehydrated a couple of personal hygiene wipes and cleaned my face, hands, arms, and legs.

17:00.   A quick trip to the Internet tent was also on my agenda, just to let my family know that I was ok. I waited in a short line before writing my message, which was limited to 1,000 words. And only one email per person was allowed, though you could queue up again as many times as you wanted, but I wanted to get off my feet, so I wrote my single email before heading back "home" to tent 40 to lie down.

By then the rest of the tent members had also returned. Fernando asked me how it was and how long I took to finish. He was impressed with my time and started saying, "Meep, meep!" in reference to the Road Runner. This ended up being his nickname for me during that week. I was flattered. Beatrice and I were also given nicknames from the guys in the Danish tent next to us—we were "Salt & Pepper."

We later found out that the 10.5-hour time limit on that days' race had been extended due to the sandstorm, otherwise another 22 people would have already been disqualified on the first day on top of the 18 who abandoned for other reasons.

Everyone began recalling tales of the day and starting to prepare the evening meals. I had a dehydrated camping meal of Vegetable Jambalaya with me. I simply added water and set it out into the sun to "cook." After about 45 minutes I was ready to eat, and it seemed to be cooked through, but the cramping in my stomach an hour later told me that maybe boiling water was actually necessary to make the food edible. Oh, well. I had a full stomach, and the calories would be absorbed.

Runners can receive emails from friends and family back home on a daily basis. We can't read them on a computer, rather they are printed out and delivered to us in our tent each night. A cherished luxury provided by the organization. A stack of pages were delivered to us that evening, and I distributed them to my tentmates; unfortunately, there were none for me. Was it possible that no one wrote? No, I was sure that my husband and kids would write, and lots of other friends had also asked beforehand how to do it via the MdS website, so I knew there must have been a mix up with the tent number and delivery. Maybe because I had switched tents? Besides, Beatrice received an email from my husband! My tentmates were laughing and absolutely overjoyed at hearing from home. Since the emotions were too overwhelming for me, especially after having such a hard day in the race, I decided that I had to leave the tent for a little while and try to find out what happened to my email. I went to the American tent that I was originally in, but they had nothing for me, so I went to the Internet tent and found a very sympathizing young woman who said that unfortunately no more emails could be printed out that night due to major technical difficulties from the sandstorm, but she wrote down my tent and start number and promised to personally see to it that my emails from both that day and the next would be delivered to me the following night. It was some consolation, and there was nothing more I could do.

19:00. I examined the Road Book to study the course for the following day—where the water rations were, whether there were dunes, villages, or a large climb. The sun began to set which provided us with some spectacular photos of a bright orange sky and the sun descending behind the mountains.

20:00. Time for bed. After the first night in the tent I knew I'd be getting very little sleep over the week. The ground was not a soft sandy surface as we envision the desert must be. Locations for the camp had to be chosen on hard flat ground. Yes, very hard, and the thin rug does little to dampen it. There are uneven places and random stones which, as luck would have it, normally protruded into your hip or shoulder. Once you wake it is hard to fall back asleep again due to the discomfort, the wind, snoring all around, or taking a peek from out of your sleeping bag and being mesmerized by the beautiful stars that brightly light up the sky all the way down to the horizon. After strolling through the camp that day, I wondered why I was the only one without a mattress. I was still bothered by not having at least a very thin foam pad to sleep on. Coach said I didn't need one. The carpets were thick, he said. They must be using different rugs this year, I thought, because I really didn't consider one centimeter to be "thick." So after the first night of tossing and turning, with my back and hips aching from the hard ground, I needed another solution. Thankfully Beatrice's short frame didn't require anywhere near the two meters of the foam fold-up mat that she brought, and after seeing me lying on the hard ground, she cut off a section of her mat that was large enough for my shoulders all the way to my hips. Much better. Then I tucked myself into my sleeping bag, drew the drawstrings, and hoped for the slumber I needed to heal my body as much as possible before I had to get up and do it again.

Sunset over the bivouac
© MARATHON DES SABLES 2016

CHAPTER 10

MY FAVORITE RACE

Oftentimes pushing the limits of your body doesn't lead to suffering, but rather the opposite. An adrenaline rush, a state of euphoria, the runner's high. This happens to me more often when I am running hilly or mountainous trails where you have a frequent change in level of difficulty, such as uphill vs. downhill, and where the terrain is uneven so that you are using a variety of muscles in your feet and legs. One of the best examples of this was years ago during my very first Alpine race, the Zugspitz Extremberglauf. And even though it was an enormous physical challenge, never have I had so much fun in a race. It was a day I'll never forget.

It's not a very long race, only about 16 kilometers (10 miles), and is run from the valley in Garmisch-Partenkirchen up to the top of the highest mountain in Germany, the Zugspitze.

Admittedly, I was nearly in tears from fear at the starting line. The 2,962-meter (9,718 feet) Zugspitze was looming over us, tempting us to try to conquer her. I wasn't confident that I could do it. Well,

I knew I would finish, but not without enduring agony along the way. But some things don't always turn out as expected.

Granted, the first five kilometers were torturous. Steeply graded, serpentine curves, heart rate over 170, full sun, 25 degrees Celsius (77 °F). Most of the runners were walking by the second kilometer. What should I do? A 176 pulse over nearly three hours is not going to work, but walking already? No way. I pushed on and passed dozens of runners who probably looked at me and thought, "Novice." True. I was a novice. That was my first mountain race, but I knew that I was well trained, and if others could do it, then so could I.

An acquaintance who'd run it the year before had given me some advice: "Try to run at least to the second alm (mountain pasture); at that point you can walk if you have to." I tried to abide by this, and for the most part I did, aside from a few short bouts of walking at the refreshment stations to bring my heart rate down. For ambitious runners it is really critical to run as much as possible in the beginning of mountain races in order to get into a fast group when you get to the single-track trails, otherwise you may find yourself slowed to a pace that doesn't allow you to run in your natural rhythm, plus you would be constantly trying to pass people, not to mention lining up at hard-to-traverse sections.

Rounding a steep curve through the second alm I passed a man who said, "Du bist eine kleine Bergziege!" (You are a little mountain goat!) I laughed, and when I saw him later at the finish he again called me a "Bergziege!"

The alms were out of a storybook where the most magnificent color of green imaginable was like a tapestry covering the hillside over which strayed free-roaming milk cows completely uninterested in our plight. After the second refreshment station, the single-track trails started, and with them the technical part of the race. The course was steep, and every step had to carefully calculated, as the "path" (for lack of a better term to describe a general patchwork of worn areas), was riddled with rocks and washed out to varying depths from rain. Passing was possible in some areas but had to be well planned. For the most part I had maneuvered into a good group, and we were running where we could and hiking at a good pace where running was not possible, either due to the grade or to other hindrances such as boulders which required all-fours to get over or around.

This style of racing was refreshing. The first five kilometers had been agony, but now the variety provided an amazing switch-off between exertion and recovery. A little hiking, pushing off against the quadriceps on the extremely steep sections, and when it flattened out, picking up the pace and running as far and as fast as possible before being slowed again by the obstacles of the mountain. At one point a few hikers alongside the trail called out my name, which was printed on my start number; I simply let out a howl in return, which was followed by, "Oh! An American!" I replied without turning around, "You can tell I'm American from my yell??" To which I heard laughing from the runners behind me.

Then the most awesome section of the race had arrived. A steep downward slope, which first started off covered in mud and with a safety rope to help us keep our balance, after which the pack of runners had to choose between a snowy field or a grassy slope of extremely uneven terrain, both at a very steep downward incline. I chose the grass, figuring it would be a safer bet, albeit a little slower. We were scattered across the area, scurrying down the hill, laughing and yelling like kids. The euphoria was all-encompassing.

The next hurdle, the remains of yet another minor avalanche, created about a 10-meter long section of parallel paths in the snow that mimicked cross-country ski tracks, and since it was steep with no place for secure footing, all you could do was step into the imprints, hold steady with arms out to your sides, let gravity take control, and just slide!

After balancing along a ridge for a while, we came up against a rock wall. About ten runners were waiting ahead to climb over it, so I had a brief chance to catch my breath. To the left was a cable mounted into the rock for us to hold on to and to the right, well...let's not go there. I just kept my focus straight ahead. Once over the "wall," the terrain was very tricky: bedrock with scattered boulders. This was the character of the trail for quite a while, almost until Knorrhütte, with occasional dirt and grassy trail sections where passing, when well calculated, was possible.

Knorrhütte was the last refreshment station, and I took a couple of glasses of water as well as an isotonic drink, but kept right on moving. From here on up it got steep. For the most part you had to stay on the trail because it was a debris field, from pebble- to baseball-sized stones, and every step onto the stones caused you to simply roll back. Staying in line on the worn trail was really the only option. And the incline was so treacherous that running was next to impossible for the first kilometer; we all took on the mountain-climber gait: long steps and pushing off from our quadriceps. Then things evened out a bit so that we could run, but another obstacle came into play: snow! The last three kilometers were a complete snow-covered trail. Passing meant wet feet. So I got wet feet.

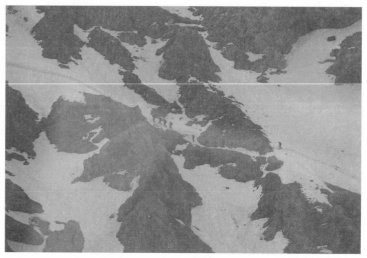

Running on the Zugspitze

Several kilometers earlier, just after the "wall," a very young Norwegian woman (we talked at the finish) had passed me, and now I had caught up to her. She clearly still had some energy and was trying to pass whenever possible, so I stayed in her footsteps and followed her moves...to the surprise of many of the male runners. "Hier kommen die Frauen!" (Here come the ladies!). And "Ihr denkt warscheinlich, dass wir Weicheier sind!" (You probably think that we are weaklings!) We laughed, and I responded that we were just in a hurry to get to the free beer at the finish.

Actually, I was thirsty. And then I realized that I was surrounded by H_2O. Ok, not in fluid form, but the snow would have to do. From the steep hillside to my right I kept grabbing handfuls of snow mid-run and slipping it in my mouth, down my shirt, and on my head. Thanks, Mother Nature. We were all still in a relatively tight pack, and at one point I briefly lost my footing in the snow and immediately felt a hand on my derriere, stopping me from falling farther. Oh my!

Just before crossing the finish line on the Zugspitze

Up over another ridge and all at once, in the distance, the finish was in sight! Really? It's almost over? Am I happy or sad that it's nearly at an end? I heard the announcer calling off finishing times, and they were coming in at around 2:45. I wanted to make it under 3 hours, but wasn't sure what the distance was and how long it would take. So I kept passing. And slipping. And running. And enjoying every moment. I suddenly heard the voice of my daughter, Sophie, from the crowd, cheering me on. I couldn't tell exactly where she was, so I waved generally to her direction. And then all at once, after a steep rocky embankment, the finish line was there...about 10 meters in front of me! I crossed over it in 2:51.33, a finisher's medal was placed around my neck, then I raised both hands in the air and, looking over to the celebrating crowd and my cheering family, let out a champion's yell! It had been me versus the mountain, and as far as I was concerned, I'd just won.

CHAPTER 11

MDS STAGE 2

ERG ZNAIGUI TO OUED MOUNGARF, 41.3 KM

5:30. We woke to a clear sky which soon turned bright blue with full sun no longer filtered by sand in the air. It was hotter than the same time the day before. My legs were heavy. I was tired because I hadn't slept well. Would today be as tough as yesterday? The route was 7 kilometers longer, albeit without the high dunes, but whether that was an equal tradeoff was yet to be seen.

8:30. Runners gathered together at the starting line. The same ritual from the day before took place. Patrick Bauer on top of the SUV. Announcements. Checkpoints. Water rations. Birthdays. Highway to Hell. Then the starting command and...nothing. No one moved. The music was so loud that the runners at the front had not heard the GO! Those behind all started yelling, but it was a good

10 seconds, with the runners and Bauer yelling over and over again, before the front of the pack started to move.

Crossing very runnable terrain
© MARATHON DES SABLES 2016

The course was flatter today. Normally I like some hills because it changes up the level of effort—sections of hard work going uphill and then regeneration going down. Just like in the Alps. Flat is monotonous and, well, boring. There was a long section in a dried-out river bed that I was lucky enough to enter just behind two other runners, Elisabeth from the Netherlands and Christopher from France (names and countries were on the start number). They were clearly running together, and I tucked up behind them with Christopher in front, who was also giving us some good draft protection since there was a strong headwind. The tempo was faster than I would have run on my own, but following someone meant that I didn't have to keep my eyes up ahead but instead simply watch each step, which was a little tricky since there was very uneven ground and quite a bit of camel grass. So I concentrated on just keeping up the pace. After a while Elisabeth switched to the front position, and I was worried that it would eventually be my turn and that I would not be able to do them justice with the pace. But after a while Elisabeth slowed to a walk (she told me later that she needed to take salt tablets), and I kept on running alone, albeit a little slower.

9:45.   Checkpoint 1 at kilometer 11.5. Two bottles of water. I filled both of my large bottles and also my small one as the next checkpoint wasn't until kilometer 26. Those 14 kilometers in between would be long and who knew what to expect with the terrain and weather. And why did it seem that regardless of which direction we ran there was always a headwind?

We occasionally passed through remote villages where children were waiting on the outskirts to give high fives and cheer us on, but I'd been warned about the transfer of germs and tried to greet them as friendly as possible without having physical contact. The risk of getting sick had me scared and on high alert!

After about 20 kilometers, which contained some not insignificant climbs, I finally got rid of the heavy legs. The hills had put some spirit into my step, and I was feeling good.

While traversing some medium-sized dunes at about kilometer 25, where running was possible but slow, I came up behind a pair that were walking and deep in discussion. The woman was tall with long legs and she wore really short shorts, actually they were "hot pants," which of course I hadn't seen on any other female runner but on her long legs and great figure they looked fantastic.

Was this a mirage? As I got closer I saw her start number with the name *Laurence* and the country *France*. Oh, my gosh! It was Laurence Klein. She is a world-class ultrarunner and has won the MdS three times in recent years. Why was I passing her? Why was she walking?

11:45. Checkpoint 2 at kilometer 26. Water bottles, salt tablets, protein bar. That was now my routine.

13:30. Checkpoint 3 at kilometer 34.5. The winds were still howling. The terrain was flat, but we were running through an oued (dried river bed) that was laden with deep sand. We tried to keep to the edges or even off the track, where the ground was a little bit harder and we could run, but it was still tough going. There were very few runners around me, but when Pierre from France passed me, I got in behind him and followed his footsteps. This was something that I loved about this race. You would often run with someone—in front, behind, or next to them—for significant distances and not even exchange a single word. It was silent companionship. The sense of security this provided in a foreign environment under extreme conditions was not to be underestimated. Pierre knew I was there and finally, after a long while, if I missed a step or changed my breathing rhythm, he'd say, "Everything alright, Holly?" in his thick French accent. There was a small gorge that we had to climb down, then a short jump across a dried-out stream bed, and finally up the other side. This was where I came too close to a thorny tree and got hung up. I mean, seriously caught. I could not move forward or backward. A branch had grabbed onto my backpack and would not let me go.

Thankfully at this time there was someone right behind me (a Scotsman) who was kind enough to take a minute to free me; otherwise I would have had to try to remove my backpack to break myself loose.

Just as I was free and climbed over the next hill I found Pierre sitting on the ground, examining his shoe. I stopped to see what was wrong, and apparently he had stepped on a thorn which had punctured his sole right through to his foot! He was trying to remove it but couldn't, so I gave it a try with my fingernails, but it wouldn't budge. Pierre told me to go on, so hesitantly I did. I knew that we were only a few kilometers from the finish so at the worst case he could make it there at a walk, but not a minute later he overtook me again and remained within sight ahead of me until crossing the finish line, where we greeted each other with a congratulatory high five.

14:50. I took the 18th place woman's finish that day. Getting better!

There was a webcam positioned at the finish line that sent live footage over the MdS website. I went straight up to it and waved (to my family), blew kisses, and gave the thumbs-up sign. Frank would later tell me in his emails that he and the kids saw me, and that made me so happy! So I consciously took a moment each time I crossed the finish line to go up to the camera and give my family some reassurance that I was alright, even if I was in rough shape. They took photos and videos on the computer monitor when I was in sight, which were a great memento when I got home.

I was feeling good as I got back to the tent, so after removing my pack and briefly resting I decided to try to prepare the ground myself. But it was riddled with small sharp stones. It would be a huge job to clear it. Thankfully, the Jalla-Jallas were out and about in masses that afternoon. These were local men and teenagers hired by the organization to set up, take down, and control the tents. Their main language was French, but there was apparently some Arabic mixed in because they were constantly yelling "Jalla-Jalla" to one another when working; we were told this means "Hurry up!" or "Let's go!" So that became their nickname. They came by and offered to help once they saw how pathetically I was trying to clear away the stubborn stones. They took off their hard, plastic flip-flops and got down on their knees and began pushing aside the debris. It was done in no time at all, and then they dropped down the "wall" of one side of the tent where the wind was blowing in, and my home was complete. Since there were only five of us in a tent that could accommodate eight people, the rug was a little longer than we required, so we would fold it over a bit on the ends to have a double layer underneath us. Because Beatrice and I shared half the tent and the guys were on the other, we had a little more leeway. I folded the rug over about 1.5 meters, still close quarters, but wide enough for both of us, and by now Beatrice and I were bosom buddies, and the closeness during the night was a comfort for us both.

15:30. I knew I needed to take in some protein, so I put a tablespoon of chia seeds into my bottle and added water. After a few minutes it turned into a gel, and I chugged it. Some salted nuts and water, and I felt like new!

16:00. Today I needed a shower. So improvisation was called upon. Mike had seen someone punching small holes into a water bottle top, and when the bottle was turned upside-down and squeezed, it mimicked a showerhead. I modified a top, grabbed my small bar of soap, two of the compressed mini-towels that I'd brought, and headed to the ladies changing stall. There were a few of these set up around the perimeter of the camp, intermittingly between the "toilets." They were simply a heavy plastic drape set up as a cubicle in which a plastic crate platform was placed, offering some drainage. These cubicles were not really provided for showers, but rather so women could have some privacy if they needed it. But with peeing in public and the all but nonexistent discretion at the toilets, they were rarely used.

But what if a woman was menstruating? This was one of my concerns in the months leading up to the race. In an Excel spreadsheet where I monitored my cycle, I watched in dread as the months passed and realized that my period was scheduled to appear on exactly the 8th of April, perfectly timed for the start of the race. So, at the end of January I made a trip to my gynecologist and said I needed to "alter my cycle." He prescribed a birth control pill for me and told me when and how long to take it. But just days after starting it, I began having extreme fatigue. Naturally, I attributed it to the intense training schedule, not to mention my work, taking care of the kids, and all the household chores. I began taking naps. Then the naps got longer and longer until I'd spend the afternoon just lying on the couch. Two weeks after starting on the pill, at the beginning of February, two months before the MdS, I planned to run a training marathon but contemplated quitting after just 10 kilometers. I couldn't hold the tempo and knew something was fundamentally wrong with my body, though at the time I didn't attribute it to the pill. I have never experienced a race like it—ever. A personal best time was the plan, and the expectations of my coach were realistic. I had never been in such good form as I'd been working on both endurance and speed for the MdS. I should have been like an angry bull in the starting block as the gun went off, but instead, the gunshots for the 10K a short time before the marathon start had me so startled, they brought me back to the finish line of Boston three years before where the explosion of two bombs instantly changed my life as well as hundreds of other runners and spectators around me, and I was briefly reduced to a basket case. But I quickly got back to the present and the start of the race was fun; I moved with the flow of the runners and settled into a five-minute pace, consistent with the expectations of my coach. There were some narrow sections where we were joggling for position within the first few kilometers, but nothing different from any other race...except that I felt as though I was "working." That feeling, for an ultrarunner, should not come for at least three hours when running at the aerobic level. I felt like we were constantly running uphill although we were actually on a slight descent.

What was wrong? I didn't know. I fought it and pushed on until kilometer 10, and then I couldn't fight it anymore. I was exhausted. I didn't even have the desire to fight it and thought about stopping, which I have never done in a race and had never even considered before!

I checked my heart rate, and my pulse read 170 BPM! Could that be true? I was running with a friend, and we slowed the pace from 5:00 min/km (8 min/mile) to 5:30 (8:50), though my pulse was still exorbitantly high, which led me to believe that my watch was not registering right. But still...something was wrong. My friend and I talked about what to do. I suggested running the half marathon and then quitting; he suggested we run 30 kilometers at our reduced pace of 5:30 so we'd still have a good Sunday long jog in the bag. I agreed.

Things did not get worse. Which isn't to say they got better. But as my long-distance training pushes me into the realms of endurance, it was clear that the reduced pace put me far back into my aerobic threshold where I could stay for hours. But still...I was exhausted. I stopped briefly at refreshment stations to drink. I never stop during races, not even ultras.

I am a thinker, and I couldn't stop trying to wrap my head about what was going on. Why was I struggling? Plausible reasons flashed through my mind:

1. I was bordering on overtraining.
2. My six-day taper was not enough.
3. The mealy potatoes and sparse salad leaves for dinner at the hotel the night before and the roll for breakfast didn't provide nearly enough energy for a walk in the park let alone a marathon.
4. The activities with the kids on school vacation the week before had me exhausted.
5. The birth control pills that I had started taking a week before to alter my menstruation so that it would not coincide with the Marathon des Sables had set my body into tumult.

All were plausible, and certainly all played their roles, but really I felt as though there was something fundamentally wrong with the way my body was functioning. There was something elemental that was causing this lack of energy and the fatigue I'd been experiencing for the past several weeks—when, for the first time in my life, I was inexplicably needing naps!

I finished in 3 hours 51 minutes; a whopping 21 minutes slower than my goal. But still a Boston Qualification...though I was not celebrating. I was cold almost immediately as I usually am after races, and I grabbed my checked bag and put on my jacket. That wasn't enough for me as I was still shivering, so I got one of the aluminum survival sheets they were passing out and wrapped it tightly around me, while forcing down fluids and some fruit.

I nearly fell asleep on the 1-hour, 20-minute drive home. After I arrived and relayed the highlights of the weekend to my family, I lay down on the couch and dozed off while my husband prepared dinner. I woke to eat, but then went straight to bed and slept for 10 hours. Monday went by in a daze, and I was a complete zombie, barely able to function. At noon I lay down for some quick shuteye and woke up a full hour later, having to force myself to get out of bed. I had to renege on taking my son to his ice hockey practice, and going to my yoga class in the evening was not an option. I was exhausted. Early to bed again and finally on Tuesday morning I felt as though I was seeing the light at the end of the tunnel.

But not really. I still needed naps the whole week, and eight days later, still feeling exhausted, I decided to pay a visit to Dr. Möckel.

Dr. Frank Möckel is a doctor specializing in sports physiology. His first instinct was an iron deficiency, which I have had trouble with in the past (see the appendix in this book for more information on iron deficiencies in distance runners). He didn't seem to think I was overtraining nor that the pill was involved with my fatigue, and he ordered a blood test. If ferritin levels (iron storage) were low, then I'd have my answer. If not, then I had trouble, because we would have to dig deeper.

I got the results, and all my values were fine. Now what? My only hope was that it was the pill because I could easily remedy that situation. I called my gynecologist who devised a plan to get me off the pill but still divert my period from appearing in the desert. Then I stopped taking it. And three days later I was back to normal, no more fatigue, no more naps, and thankfully, no bleeding in the desert.

Back in Morocco and the shower—I got undressed and sprayed myself with a trickle of water from head to toe. We needed to carefully watch our water usage as the rations were to be used for drinking, cooking, and cleaning. Additional water could be acquired if necessary, but they were assigned with a time penalty. So I made due with what we were allotted. There was not enough water to wash my hair, but I gave my body a good scrubbing and also washed out my race clothes. I felt like a new person. Then off to the Internet tent to send a message back home.

16:45.   When I got back to the tent, there was still no one there. But only a few minutes later, Mike returned. He was in good spirits but clearly exhausted. He was relieved and happy to see the tent was ready, and he could simply lie down and relax. I did the same, elevating my feet almost perpendicularly upwards on one of the tent stability poles. I wanted to reduce the minor swelling that had begun in my ankles. And soon after I was thrilled to see that my emails had arrived! Four pages of them!

17:45.   Another hour had passed before Cap and Fernando arrived. The two of them were walking the entire course and enjoying much needed quality time together since they live continents apart. Fernando said that walking the distance was actually more difficult than running it, because you are outside in the hot sun for nearly twice the time but still expending a lot of energy. The two of them were in good shape and in high spirits. Are all Brazilians always so happy? But where was Beatrice?

18:15. Half an hour later she arrived, and she didn't look good. She was very quiet and weak. She said she was having a sugar low. We were all worried and immediately went into action. I took off her shoes and gaiters, then prepared her mattress and sleeping bag while the guys started a fire and began boiling water for her dinner. We tried to get her to drink and take salt tablets and keep her as positive as possible. After a hot meal and a good night's sleep she would be good as new, we told her. But in the state that she was in, we were not convinced ourselves. She ate her meal while shivering in her sleeping bag and thick jacket. The whole time she never once complained nor mentioned the idea of giving up.

That night I checked my feet and had a few blisters. Not surprising considering the conditions. I had taken some effort prior to the race to treat my feet with sprays and creams, and I thought that they were in good shape, but running through deep, soft sand requires an incredible amount of toe effort. With every step the toes are constantly asked to keep the body in balance. I could feel them working inside my shoes all day long, and though the gaiters worked wonders in keeping the sand out, and the toe socks kept the digits from rubbing directly against one another, and my shoes two sizes larger accommodated the swelling, it was still too much for my little piggies. There were two blisters on the toes of my left foot. I didn't think these required a trip to the clinic, so I simply popped them myself and then applied topical antiseptic. *Ouch!*

20:00. I studied the Road Book, brushed my teeth with my sawed-off toothbrush, then eagerly climbed into my sleeping bag. The air was still warm, so I only had a T-shirt on and not my light fleece jacket, but during the night this always changed. At around 3am it would suddenly get cold, and I would have to put on the extra layer. I am sure that my constant state of physical exhaustion played a role in regulating my body temperature. I'd soon learn that it could get worse: Cold temps plus a

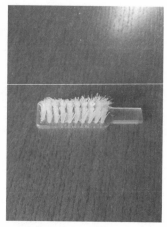
My sawed-off toothbrush

sandstorm in an open tent were not part of the equation for a good night's rest. Our routine each night before we went to sleep was to drop some tent poles against the direction of the incoming wind, but if the tent wasn't closed properly on one side, or if the wind direction changed, then we had a wind tunnel effect, and all you could do was pull the sleeping bag drawstring tight and hunker down.

21:00. Beatrice was sleeping soundly. Again, I lay awake for a long time. My hips and back hurt, and Cap was snoring loudly. Oh, well, guess it was a good time to peek outside the tent to see a sky full of bright stars that reached to the horizon and enjoy being lulled to sleep by the wonders of the heavens. The cost was indeed high, but the benefits were priceless.

CHAPTER 12

BEST FEMALE RUNNERS AND CLINICAL EXERCISE TESTING

I was happy with my performance on that second day. Before the race it was almost impossible for me to predict where I would end up in that field of both world-elite and kickass hobby runners. But naturally I was hoping to surprise myself.

The previous year I underwent a clinical exercise test, which was originally spurred by my iron deficiency…although that may have been my ~~excuse~~ reason to finally get it done, since I was really curious about where some of my values stood.

I headed to Dr. Frank Möckel for spiroergometry testing 12 months before the race. All I had to do was mention the Marathon des Sables, and he immediately understood why I was there. He himself is a runner and an avid adventurer, with many impressive mountain treks to his credit, so I know I'm in good hands when it comes to talking sports medicine with him.

Alright then, so, what exactly is spiroergometry? (And how is that even pronounced?) Well, it is a type of stress test whereby you breathe through a mask while running on a treadmill (or riding a stationary bike or using a rowing machine) in order to measure oxygen input and carbon dioxide output. The test simultaneously employs the ECG (electrocardiography), allowing assessment of cardiopulmonary performance in addition to evaluating the blood pressure and heart rate under stress. This test is used to determine oxygen consumption and anaerobic threshold in combination with determining your lactate values. The ultimate goal is essentially (for athletes) to determine the correct intensity for base, recovery, and intense interval training.

Next question. What is lactate and what are lactate values? Lactate refers to lactic acid which is a carboxylic acid with the chemical formula $C_2H_4OHCOOH$ (ok, yes, that is beyond the scope of this book). During power exercises such as sprinting, when the rate of demand for energy is high, glucose is broken down and oxidized to pyruvate, and lactate is produced from the pyruvate faster than the tissues can remove it, which is when lactate concentration begins to rise, increasing incrementally with exercise intensity. When you achieve a certain intensity where lactate increases exponentially, you are crossing the lactate (or aerobic) threshold. This is also sometimes referred to as "hitting the wall" in a marathon. There is not sufficient glucose to feed the muscles, and the acid buildup essentially forces the muscles to stop working. Fatigue onset is rapid above the lactate threshold (LT), but efforts just below the LT can be sustained for hours by well-trained athletes.

Lactate values in the blood measured during spiroergometry help determine the correct training intensity to increase power and endurance. That said, it is important to know these values so that training can be done efficiently and effectively. At either end of the exercise intensity extremes, the result is the same: lots of exercise but poor or inconsistent results.

Back to the doc...So, after a slurry of questions, Dr. Möckel hooked me up to a heart-rate belt and another bazillion cables and took me out to the treadmill. There I was also strapped into a harness mounted from above—in case I tripped while running, I would be whisked up into the air rather than fall flat on my face.

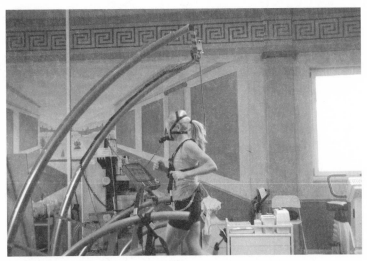

Spiroergometry testing

After about a 10-minute warm-up jog, the test began. The pace to start was an easy 8.0 kilometers (5 miles) per hour sustained for three minutes, after which the technician stopped the treadmill, took a quick blood sample from my earlobe (*ouch!*), and then sent me immediately on my way again at a 10 km/hr (6 miles/hr) pace. Three minutes; blood sample; 12 km/hr. Repeat at 14, then

16 km/hr (10 miles/hr), which I could not maintain for the full three minutes, and the test was over. *Ta da!*

After a shower I was back in the doctor's office with a multitude of datasheets in front of me. "You are healthy!" he happily announced. Uhh, yeah. Right. Thanks, doc...what is this appointment costing me? But then we got down to the nitty-gritty and examined my values, talked about my upcoming goals, and then decided how I should go about training to achieve them.

"What is your breathing schedule?" he asked me.

Is this a trick question, I wondered? "Um, well, regularly," I answered. Yep, that seems to work best for me.

He smiled. "No, when running, how many steps per breath?"

Oh. "I don't know. Whatever it takes."

He said I was using too much air. What? Thank goodness there is an endless supply, was my thought. Apparently, I was using about 2 liters per minute more than I should be, or more than most runners do. This may sound insignificant, but when running for hours on end, it could amount to an extraordinary waste of energy. His recommendation to improve this was to practice controlled breathing during regeneration runs: breathe in, four steps; breathe out, four steps.

One really cool value was my VO_2max, which is reached when the volume of oxygen consumed is equal to the volume of CO_2 exhaled and is essentially a measure of potential speed and endurance—the higher the value, the greater your potential. My value was higher than I thought. But whether I could use those numbers to guide my training and improve my performance enough to be competitive with some of the world's best trail runners remained to be seen.

A short time later, an article came out on the Marathon des Sables website entitled "Best Female Runners." I was so excited to read about the incredible women I'd encounter in Morocco, and I read through the list of favorites in awe. What I didn't expect to see, naturally, was my name on that list, but there it was.

I had to look twice.

At the bottom of the page were several "Long Shots" listed according to country, and there, under United States, were two names, and one of them was mine.

Race history was not provided upon registration, so obviously some Internet searching had been done to check up on the runners. I was completely humbled and very motivated to have my name in the company of these world-class athletes.

Though, I have to admit, I checked back on the article several times just to make sure I wasn't dreaming or that there was some kind of mistake, and my name had been subsequently removed. Or maybe there was a second Holly Zimmermann running, too? Nope, it must be me, so I took some photos of the computer screen.

Realistically my chances of winning the lottery were as good as being up on the podium at the MdS, but still, if you believe in yourself, incredible things can sometimes happen.

CHAPTER 13

MDS STAGE 3

OUED MOUNGARD TO BA HALLOU, 37.5 KM

5:30. Why do people wake up this early? The camp began to awake at this god-forsaken hour every day, which was when I went into denial and slid deeper into my sleeping bag where it was dark and safe to try to get a few more winks before sunrise.

6:00. Same ritual: eat breakfast, get dressed, prepare food for the day, pack backpack, collect water, fill bottles, walk of shame

Volunteers from the organization came by each morning and sometimes in the afternoons to give us information and personally see how we were doing. I didn't learn many of their names, but some of their faces I will never forget. We were told that during stage 2 another 52 runners were forced to abandon the race.

Seventy in total after two days? That was abnormally high, and they attributed it to the weather conditions—the wind had been brutal both days.

I had enough water from the night before to fill both of my water bottles for the race, including a bit extra to drink in the morning. For that reason, I didn't collect the extra 1.5 liters that was provided at water rations that morning. The Road Book said the first checkpoint was at kilometer 10.6, so 1.4 liters of water should be plenty, right? But soon the temperature began to rise, and I realized it was warmer than the previous days, plus there was no wind. I had drunk my extra water and was getting thirsty as the time neared to approach the starting line. I realized then that I may have made a mistake by not taking the extra rations. The 10 kilometers to the first checkpoint could take anywhere between 1.5 and 2 hours, depending on terrain, and one of my rules of thumb was to drink one bottle (700ml) per hour, regardless of distance. Many people who use the large front-pocket attachment of the MdS backpack from WAA have a pouch that holds a 1.5-liter bottle of water. As I wasn't using this front pocket, I didn't have anywhere to hold an extra bottle, and I couldn't carry such a large bottle in my small hand anyway. For that reason, I saved a half-liter bottle from my stay at the hotel in Ouarzazate and carried that as an extra water supply in my hand until it was empty, and then I could easily tuck it into the side bands on my backpack. This meant I could carry almost two liters of water at one time, which, even at that large amount, I was cutting it close sometimes between checkpoints.

8:30. Start. I was thirsty. Beatrice had both her water bottles full plus an extra 1.5-liter full bottle from which she forced me to drink once I mentioned that I was already thirsty and was worried about my water supply. And thankfully she was feeling much better—actually, she was as good as new from the previous night! She said she slept very well, a full 9 hours, and she was full of energy. We were all so relieved!

There was almost no wind. It was very hot and dry, 42 degrees Celsius (108 °F) and 5% humidity, as I'd later learned. The terrain was relatively flat, but there was a lot of sand so that I had to do a lot of walking. I don't like walking; it was just as much effort for me to walk as a slow jog, and it was just too hot to spend that much time out in the desert. It was depressing not to be progressing as fast as I wanted. But I had to push on. I religiously took small sips of water and kept an eye out for dehydration. I had actually developed my own technique for evaluating my level of hydration. I call it the "Elephant Skin Technique." It really can only be used by women over a certain age, about 40ish, who have already started to wrinkle, and having had children increases its accuracy. I notice that the skin on my quads tends to fall together in atrociously ugly mini-folds of wrinkles, like those of an elephant, when I am not properly hydrated. And it gets better or worse within minutes depending on how much I am drinking. I was watching it closely today, and it got slightly worse during the first couple of hours, but after my religious drinking, it began to get better. When I normally feel really good and strong, the skin on my quads is taut and lovely. I've since looked up "elephant wrinkles" to see if there is actually anything more to my theory than the visual similarity, and surprisingly, there is! Apparently African elephants have baggy skin to keep them cool in the hot sun, whereby moisture is trapped in the hollows, making it take longer to evaporate, thus keeping the elephant cooler for longer. Ok, well, maybe I didn't have much moisture collection in my quad furrows, but the theory still worked well enough for me.

Hydration under control
© MARATHON DES SABLES 2016

9:45. Checkpoint 1. Two bottles of water. Relief.

10:45. There was a steep climb up a stony gorge at kilometer 17 to reach the peak of the Foum Al Opath jebel. There were some large flat stones in a path that cut up the mountainside and looked like it had been an ancient stream or even an old Roman road. But the path was rather congested, and we were slowed to a walk. The peak was high above me, and I could see runners assembled there, briefly enjoying the view. Once I arrived, I realized it was probably more of a much deserved break rather than enjoying the vista that kept the runners there. From on top I could see small black objects in the valley below. I only paused for a moment before descending on the other side through deep sand laden with football-sized rocks. As I ran on, I realized that those dark spots I had seen from above were goats that were being tended by several young children. Where the heck do those kids live? We did not pass through or near any villages that day. I considered how different their culture was from ours. Would I ever let my 8-year-old go that far from home alone?

11:30. I needed a toilet. Peeing was easy, I could do that anywhere, but I wasn't ready to have a bowel movement in the path of hundreds of runners. Someone had told me in past years there were toilets at the checkpoints. So at CP2, kilometer 23.5, I asked where the toilets were. I was told there were none, and I just had to find a "spot." Oh, great. It's not like there are a lot of trees and bushes in the desert, and going far off the path, into scorpion territory, was less appealing to me than enduring the stomach pressure for the next 3 hours. But eventually I found myself in relative solitude, and a small tree surrounded by camel grass about 50 meters off the path was my target. My toilet paper was easily accessible from the bottom zip pocket of my backpack, so I could get to it while leaving the pack on. I dug a hole with my heel and took care of business as quickly as possible, keeping an eye out for creepy-crawlies, and I was on my way again in no time flat!

Speaking of creepy-crawlies, I actually didn't come across many animals that week. There were lots of black beetles that made cute little tracks in the sand. That herd of goats tended to by children. Black camels with a herder. Small lizards. And that was it. Others saw scorpions and a big green snake on the stony mountain climb during the long stage, but I had thankfully been spared those encounters.

The last 10 kilometers were in a dry riverbed that was well packed. I could finally run again! Granted, I was exhausted, but I was so happy to be able to again get into that easy rhythm that I love. Everyone else around me was walking. I kept running and passing and running and felt better the more I ran. A few times the organization vehicles came by, waved, and asked if I was all right; each time I gave the thumbs-up. At one point, one of the cars was adjacent to me as I passed three men who were walking…I looked at the volunteers in the car, then at the walkers, and raised my shoulders in a gesture as if to say, "Why are they walking?" They laughed. Then another car accompanied me a while and talked while I ran. It made the time fly by, and soon enough, I had the finish line in sight and stage 3 checked off.

Nothing like the feeling of an easy jog
© MARATHON DES SABLES 2016

14:45. After 6 hours and 12 minutes, I had a 28th place women's finish…a little disappointing, but considering the dehydration, it could have been a lot worse.

Once I collected my water bottles and returned to the tent, I was exhausted. I removed my pack and lay down. Then I realized how much my feet were hurting, so I took off my shoes and gaiters and saw the mess that once were my feet. I tried to elevate my legs and drink some water. I prepared my chia-seed drink and also ate some salted nuts, which were the best things I had to eat in my whole pack; thankfully I had some nuts for each day. But as I lay there, the blisters on my toes and feet seemed to appear one after the other, and my ankles were swollen. As the first one back to our tent, I felt I should get to work and clean the ground, but I just did not have the energy. It would have to wait.

15:30.   Next on hand had to be a trip to the clinic. When I arrived I "took a number" and was told the wait would be 60 to 90 minutes, so I went next door to the Internet tent and wrote an email home. The Internet tent had about 15 rudimentary computers set up for us to send home emails. Before each computer was a small stool, which was the only opportunity to sit on some sort of a chair during the entire period there. Going a week without ever having the luxury of sitting on a chair was also something that I hadn't thought of beforehand. Sitting on the ground gets uncomfortable after a short period of time. An entire week—actually nine days including the two days of logistics—made one long for so many of the basic comforts of modern life that we normally take for granted.

17:00.   Back at the clinic, after washing my feet with the cleansing liquid provided, and putting on the little hospital booties, I was shown to Dr. Adrien, a very young, very cute, and very serious guy. I lay back on the ground, like the dozens of other patients in the clinic, and hoisted a foot up onto the mini tripod stool positioned before the good doctor.

I pointed five blisters out to him and mentioned that my large toenail hurt a lot. He said that there was probably a blister under it and that he would have to go underneath with a needle and pop it to release the fluid. I squeamed at the thought, then reluctantly pointed out three other toenails that hurt as well. Wouldn't you know I'd be doomed to lose all four of those toenails in the coming weeks, and although I later left the clinic with bandaged feet that looked like I just came out of a war zone, I felt much better.

Runners getting their feet attended to in the Medical Tent
© Gabriel Biguria

By the time I got back to the tent, Mike was there, and the ground was prepared!

18:00. Another four pages of emails, which I slowly savored reading as I ate my rehydrated warm meal of mashed potatoes with hemp seeds and veggies, plus, of course, lots of water. I put on my compression calf sleeves to

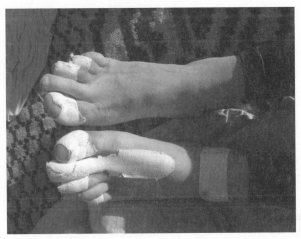

My "repaired" feet

hopefully help reduce the swelling in my ankles. I don't particularly like to run with them on, but I use them often after races. I decided I would leave them on overnight.

20:00. Study the Road Book then bedtime! Brushed my teeth under the stars, then into my sleeping bag, which was starting to feel amazingly cozy and comfortable. Perspectives can change quickly. Had to get some good sleep for the "big day," a whopping 84.3 kilometers (52 miles), a double marathon, lay await in the day ahead.

CHAPTER 14

LOSING TOENAILS

Yes, I've devoted a chapter to this topic. No, there are no photos, and it is not a long chapter, but it remains important in and of itself. Why? Because losing toenails is part of ultrarunning like a broken nose is to boxing or a concussion to football (though not quite as serious).

I've lost count of how many toenails I've sacrificed to my love of running over the years. The unthinkable phenomena of losing toenails shocked me when I'd first heard about it. Those runners must be doing unfathomable mileage or their shoes are too tight or they have calcium and vitamin D deficiencies or…something. I mean, how bizarre and gross. And painful. And icky.

But to tell the truth, it's not that bad. The toenails are damaged on a regular basis during training, and then when you race and hold nothing back, that's when you sometimes push them (actually your whole body) to the breaking point. Occasionally there is just a blister on the side of your toe or general soreness to the touch. But oftentimes there is a blood blister under the nail that needs to get punctured to relieve the pressure. That obviously takes a certain level of pain tolerance: pushing a sterilized pin underneath your toenail, popping the blister, and then squeezing out the reddish liquid. But, good news, it immediately feels better. It's similar to childbirth…absolute agony until the baby pops out then…nothing! Pain free! Although with the toenail, the damage is done, and if the nail doesn't fall off immediately, it's only a matter of time before a new nail starts to grow and push the old one out. The big toenail comes off clean, like a sheet of paper, but the baby toes are the worst. You'd think they fall out as such cute little things, like a delicate contact lens or pinkie finger nail, but don't be deceived, they are more like a big chunk of calcium accumulation or a badass baby tooth!

I love to torment my kids with the condition of my feet after a race. "Come here and look at this!" I'd say pulling off my sock. They used to fall for it, but not anymore, though I still try to trick them into looking. Although, after an ultra, there is usually no way around it, since I've got compression socks on and, considering the state I'm in, I am not able to get them off myself…and so if my husband is not around, then whichever of my kids is in the vicinity gets the honors. Giant blisters. Sometimes dried blood. They shriek. I laugh. They still love me.

As I'm writing this, the nail on my right big toe does not look good. I lost the top nail to find two new growths beneath—both of which are already damaged! It doesn't seem to be growing back right, so I think I'll be needing some kind of artificial nail for the summer. I wear my beaten-up toenails as a badge of honor around the house…but not in public. Unfortunately that would embarrass my kids way too much.

CHAPTER 15

MDS STAGE 4

BA HALLOU TO HASSI TARFA, 84.3 KM

5:30.   Wake to the stirring of the camp, but I stay curled up
deep down in my sleeping bag for warmth and in denial
of what lay ahead. The big day had arrived. The one
we all were dreadfully anticipating, but with the first
three stages behind me successfully completed, I was
pretty sure I could get through this one, too. The MdS,
though changing its course route and distance every year,
sticks to a basic scheme whereby the first three days are
"short"—in other words, about a marathon in length—
the fourth day is a double marathon, and the fifth is again
a single marathon. Then comes the last stage which
is a charity walk that varies in length from just a few
kilometers to nearly twenty. Luck would have it that this
year it would be the latter. As a matter of fact, at a total of
257 kilometers (160 miles), it was the longest MdS in the
race's 31-year history. Rumor had it that the organization

wanted to pump up the difficulty in order to live up to its reputation of being "the toughest race on earth." The fall-out, unfortunately, was a coincidingly higher dropout rate.

6:00. Reluctantly I sat up, though still in the sleeping bag, and ate my breakfast of two BP-WRs plus half of a Millenium bar left over from the day before and some cold coffee. I began getting my backpack ready for the day, including putting all the food I would require in the small front pack. It was bulging full today as I'd need two and a half thousand calories—considerably less than I'd be burning, but hopefully enough to keep me going.

7:00. Got dressed in race clothes. Rolled up and stuffed sleeping bag into tiny little storage bag.

7:30. Collected water rations. Completed final packing. Filled water bottles.

7:45. Walk of shame.

8:00. Head to starting line. The mood in the camp was subdued; we were all very humble that morning, perhaps showing respect for our human meekness and the feat we were about to attempt.

8:15. Start. *Highway to Hell* had never been so poignant. The first 10 kilometers were flat and alternated between a hard-packed, dried-out river bed where I ran slowly and sandy sections where I walked. The 100 top finishers from the first three days would start later that morning so that every runner would have to endure part of that leg during the night, and despite the fact that the fastest were not among us, it was clear that the pack was slower than on the other days, as we were all trying to ration our energy.

9:45. Checkpoint 1: Filled water bottles. Drank. Poured water over my head and neck. Took salt tablets. Ate a small piece of a protein bar.

10:00. The beginning of the nightmare. Here's what the Road Book says about this section: "*Go W/SW (course 257°) for difficult ascent up El Otfal jebel. 12% average slope until summit, with 30% over the last 500m. Ascent alternating rocky and sandy parts.*" I mean, if the Road Book used the word "difficult," that means you should be nothing less than petrified, because there is not a thing that is NOT difficult in this race, even on the gentlest of sections!

We were packed single file on the ascent, going was slow, and climbing sometimes required using my hands. My quads were aching as I reached the

Ascent to El Otfal jebel
© Gabriel Biguria

summit, and the fabulous view from the top was not in any way a reward since all that really stood out were an extremely difficult descent, a large swath of dunes which I would have to cross once I finally reached the bottom, and bivouac 4 off to the right which I wouldn't reach for another 16 hours! The course took a figure-8 route that day which is why we could already see our path to the finish. How cruel!

11:30. After painstakingly making the descent and traversing the dunes, almost four hours had gone by since the start. My quads were aching, the heat and sun were scorching, and I'd only covered about 15 kilometers (9 miles). I still had 70 kilometers (43 miles) to go that day. This was where the mental battle began.

Sometimes descents are tougher than going up
© Gabriel Biguria

A salt flat for about 5 kilometers offered the opportunity to run, and I was joined by a young woman from London, Kat, who was a doctor in the military. This was a fabulous distraction, and we chatted away.

Then Mike ran by me. What?? He said that he was worried to see me because that meant that he was probably going too fast. I was worried that it meant that I was going too slow, but I kept that to myself. Kat stopped to walk, and I continued jogging with Mike for a while until the terrain only allowed walking due to another steep climb. Since Mike's legs go up to about my chest, his walking pace was much faster than mine, and he moved on ahead.

Jogging on a brief section of road after the salt flats
© MARATHON DES SABLES 2016

12:00. Checkpoint 2 (kilometer 21.7) Load up on water. Take salt tablets. Eat a piece of protein bar, some salty nuts. Drink, drink, drink then douse the remaining 0.5 liters of water over my neck, back, arms, and legs. Keep moving.

14:30. Shortly after checkpoint 3 (kilometer 35.2), I met Gabriel from Guatemala. We talked and talked the entire time, except when we stopped so he could take photos. To have an extended conversation with someone—first Kat and then Gabriel—was rare for me in the race because I was usually trying to save energy by not having to talk, think, etc., and also because it is hard to find someone who is moving at your own pace. But Gabriel and I were pretty much resigned to walking from there out. The sand was deep, and there were steep climbs over difficult rocky terrain, not to mention the scorching, late-afternoon sun. A few of the 100 top runners passed us, but not many. Gabriel raised shrimp in a family business, which sounds very *Forrest Gump*, which of course was my initial comment, but he actually travels around the world quite a bit, attempting to create a world market for the industry in Guatemala, and he is very eco-friendly and wise.

Gabriel from Guatemala and me
© Gabriel Biguria

17:00. Checkpoint 4 (kilometer 45.3). Gabriel and I got separated while collecting water. I had to sit and rest in the shade of one of the tents for about 15 minutes. During that time, Elisabeth Barnes, the winner from the previous year, entered the CP, after having started later with the leaders. It was her birthday, and she was greeted by several runners, though she didn't waste much time other than to refill her water supply before she was off again. I looked into the other tents for Gabriel but couldn't find him, so reluctantly I took off again on my own.

18:00. On a steep climb after CP4, I ran into Patrick Bauer and another race organizer who were coming the opposite way. Where were they coming from? We were a couple of kilometers from CP4, even more to CP5, and I saw no possibility of a vehicle getting to this location. This guy is a marvel.

19:30. At sundown, I noticed that everyone had glow sticks tucked into their backpacks. I didn't have one. I asked a guy where he got it. He was from Spain and spoke almost no English but relayed that he got it at CP4 and that maybe I could get one at CP5. Once he was out of earshot, I began to cry because I thought I might be penalized for not having a glow stick. But I never saw them at CP4! Where was I supposed to get one? I figured that it would be handed to me at water rations, but it didn't cross my mind to ask for one. It got dark, and I needed to turn on my headlamp. CP5 could be seen very far in the distance, but it seemed like an impossible eternity away. In the low light at dusk, the route was very difficult to make out. There were also glow sticks set out to mark the route every couple hundred meters or so, but they were very hard to distinguish. The terrain was sandy with mounds of small dunes and grass. It was tough to navigate; I was tired, scared, and could barely face the thought of still having 35 kilometers in front of me that day/evening/next day.

I cried until I reached the next checkpoint. I was just so exhausted that I couldn't keep the emotions inside. I'd later find out that I was not the only one who'd spent time crying that day.

20:30. Finally reached checkpoint 5 (kilometer 55.6). I saw two runners that I knew from a neighboring tent, Elisabeth (from pacing in the flats during stage 2) and Friso (who'd I'd later run with in stage 6 and who is also pictured on the front cover). Elisabeth's facial reaction when she saw me pretty much confirmed how I felt. She told me that I did not look good and that I should take a long rest. That checkpoint was set up with lounge chairs, tea, and music. Apparently, many runners spent the night there and finished the remaining 30 kilometers of the stage on the next day.

I saw Gabriel just as he was getting ready to leave. He said he was taking off with a guy from Greece if I wanted to join them, but I had only been there a few minutes and was not in any condition to go yet, which was unfortunate because I could really have used his company. I couldn't move. I was at an absolute low point—in a state that I had never been before in my life.

I drank a cup of tea, and with very slow movements, ate some of my sports bar, some nuts, and drank as much water as I could. I tried to "relax," but everything hurt. Getting up to get another cup of tea was not possible; my body ached so badly, all I could do was lie completely immobile. I thought about my family at home, wondering if they were watching my progress on the Internet tracker and if they were worried.

21:00. I had stayed for about 30 minutes; it was now or never. I got up slowly, painstakingly put my pack on, and turned to tackle the tortuously steep climb directly behind the checkpoint. It was here where I was told later by a runner that he had seen a giant scorpion. I could have walked right past hundreds of them but would have never noticed in the condition I was in.

Then, as if it couldn't get any worse, it did. The light of my headlamp started to dim. There was no way I could safely get through the terrain without light. I would have to change the batteries. It was pitch black out there. If I took out the old batteries, I'd have no light to put in the new ones; it was that dark. A catch-22. I contemplated this situation for what seemed to be an eternity. Finally, off in the distance I saw the headlights of a vehicle, an SUV from the organization, patrolling the route. I flagged them down. They asked if I was ok; of course I wasn't, but I said that I was fine, though I needed to change the batteries in my headlamp and could I please use the light of their car to do it? They were in good spirits and joking with me, but the most I could summon was a polite smile. They must have sensed my desperation, and one of them took the headlamp and spare batteries out of my fumbling hands and in no time had them changed. I was so grateful. Then he gestured as if he would throw the old batteries out into the desert. I was horrified and said, no! He laughed and said he was only kidding and put them into his pocket to dispose of them back at camp.

23:00. Arrived at CP6 (kilometer 65.9) after nearly 15 hours since starting that morning. I sat down for about 20 minutes. I had to put on my windbreaker for warmth because as soon as I stopped moving I got cold. As I started up again I was immediately warm and had to stop after only about five minutes to remove the jacket, but I knew I'd be needing it again soon at the next checkpoint. Out of habit I continued to drink water regularly, but now that it was cold and dark I didn't sweat as much, so I often had to stop to pee. Anyplace was as good a spot as any other out there. There was a long stretch for over an hour where a Chinese runner was near me, but instead of walking next to me, he was weaving all around. Sometimes 20 meters in front or behind. Back and forth across the track. I was a little worried and kept an eye on him while trying to keep a straight line myself. That actually became my main mantra for the entire race: "The shortest distance between two points is a straight line." That statement must have gone through my head a thousand times during that week. But it was not always easy to take the shortest route, as there were sometimes canyons or sand dunes that looped around, but I knew that every meter shorter to traverse was a blessing for my feet as well as reaching the finishing line.

At one point a female runner came past me. Clearly one of the late starters. I was walking. She did not say a thing as she ran right by me. On her start number was printed USA, just like mine.

1:00. Arrived at checkpoint 7, the final of the day, at kilometer 74.9. I got my water and staggered to a tent. I lay down and curled up like a baby on the rug. I stayed that way for at least 30 minutes while listening to a group of three British men next to me. They were also barely coherent but were still telling jokes, which you've got to love the Brits for. I said nothing the whole time, but was disappointed when they got up to go. Then I heard a voice right next to me, "Don't fall asleep, Holly, or you will regret it." I couldn't manage a response but looked up to see a man whose start number read: Andrew, GBR. He walked off, and I knew he was right. So I began organizing myself for the last leg of that stage.

1:45. Once I left that last checkpoint, it was not too long until I finally got lucky and found someone I could join up with: Ole, from Norway. We greeted each other weakly and walked next to each other for several minutes without saying a word, both happy that'd we found someone of the same pace.

Then, out of the blue, he said, "It's my birthday". I wished him a happy birthday, and being only 2am, there was still a chance of that happening, that it may turn "happy," though at the moment the mood was rather dim. Then in the distance we saw some lights, but they looked like they were a hundred miles away. I wondered what city or town it could be. Ole wondered if it was the finish line and our camp. Neither of us could fathom that that could be true; it just looked unrealistically far away, and we supposedly had only 9 kilometers to go. It couldn't possibly be that we still had to go that far, could it? Ole's headlamp started to dim and then finally extinguish. He had no more spares after already having used his so much during the evenings in camp. He would have to stay with me, or find another runner, in order to make his way. I walked faster with him than I would have alone, and he said the same was true for him. A win-win for us both. But those lights in the distance never seemed to get any closer; it was rather as though they kept sliding farther and farther away. But we knew we were on the right path, between the two of us it was easier to spot the course markers, and eventually we approached those lights on the distant horizon; yes, it was our next bivouac.

3:30.   Finally, after 19 hours 13 minutes and 29 seconds, I crossed the finish line. Despite a 44th place women's finish for that day, I felt like a huge winner. I briefly walked up to the webcam and waved to my family, blowing them kisses, to let them know I'd made it and was ok. I passed on the hot tea that was offered to us, instead giving mine to Ole, grabbed my water bottles, and trudged on to Tent 40.

I got back to the tent to find that Mike was there, asleep. Naturally, I wouldn't have expected that the ground was cleaned by him or anyone after such a long haul, but I also didn't expect the rug to be clearly pulled to the guys' side of the tent where it was doubled over about two meters, on top of which Mike lay asleep. Upon his blow-up mattress. Of course. There was barely enough rug on the ladies' side for two to lie, so folding the rug over was unfortunately not an option in case Beatrice showed up. I would have to lie on a single-layered rug on top of an uncleaned ground after being on my feet for over 19 hours. I was not happy, but I was also too exhausted to be angry.

4:00.   I ate some nuts, half a protein bar, and drank some water. I washed my face, hands, and feet before putting on my calf sleeves and getting into my sleeping bag. I slept for two hours.

6:30.   Quickly sneak out of my tent for a pee break, then back to the comforts of my sleeping bag for another two hours of sleep. That would have to suffice; I couldn't sleep any more. Only four hours of sleep after a double marathon.

I knew I would have to rest the entire day and hopefully get a nap in, but of course that was wishful thinking since runners were constantly coming in, and every time another finisher would wearily walk through camp, laden with backpack and carrying their three bottles of water, they were cheered on by everyone who was around. I didn't want to miss a minute of it. The comradery was beautiful; everyone suffered and sieged together.

10:00. Time for another rudimentary shower. Absolute heaven.

10:45. I ran into a woman who I'd met that first afternoon in the American tent, and we chatted for a while about the long day. Her name had also been listed in the article written about the female favorites for the MdS. I told her that she was "the other long-shot" of the American women. She was surprised and thrilled, as I had been, and from then on that was our mutual nickname: the Other Long-Shot.

11:00. Another trip to the clinic where I was told there would be a three-hour wait, so I took a number and went to the Internet tent and waited in a long line to write my single email home. Everyone was talking about how tough the long stage was. Some of the runners were comparing it with other races they'd run: Badwater, Leadville, Rim-to-Rim-to-Rim, and they all were convinced that the MdS was the toughest race they'd ever competed in; although, I'm not so sure that is true, but in our present moment of agony, it may certainly have seemed that way.

12:15. Since I still had plenty of time before my number would be called at the clinic, I went back to the tent to rest and see if any more from our group had returned. Fernando and Cap were back! They looked good, but Fernando explained how Cap had had a difficult night. He had suffered some hypothermia and his body temperature was still low. He needed food and rest.

13:15.   Beatrice finally turned up and looked as though she'd just went for a short walk in the park! What is her secret? She explained how she had met a "lovely British woman" with whom she'd spent the whole night. They cooked dinner together, well, actually the British woman had extra food and a stove and thus cooked dinner for both Beatrice and her, and they then made "camp" at CP5 and slept for five hours until sunrise before walking the remaining 30 kilometers together. A polar opposite experience from my own.

13:30.   I decided to go back to the clinic and wait, though they were still far from calling my number. I cleaned my feet, put on the medical booties, and lay down in one of the waiting tents. This was where I met Andre. There was a small free space on one of the mats where I squeezed myself into and lay next to a man who looked like he was asleep, or dead. His eyes were closed; he looked completely wiped out, but then, without moving, he spoke: "Sorry if I stink." I told him that he didn't stink, which he really didn't. We began to chat. He still had his start number on, so he obviously came to the clinic directly after finishing the race, which is also how I knew his name was Andre, and his country read RSA: Republic of South Africa. Though he went on to explain that he didn't live there; he owned two bars in St. Anton in Austria where he spent the winters, then summered on the Isle of Wight. His tent was across from mine, he said, and he was in with all French speakers, though he spoke no French himself. He said they were all very nice but not being able to communicate with them was difficult. Why was he in that tent then? Long story, he said.

My number was finally called, and it took Doc Nicolas 45 minutes to treat my plethora of blisters that had now spread to the ball of my left foot. *Ouch!*

15:00. Next stop was the communications tent to make a satellite telephone call to the radio station back home. They were expecting my call at some point that day and quickly put me through to tape. I only had a few minutes of talk time, and after explaining some of the highlights and downsides of the week, the connection was abruptly cut off. It would have to do. I needed to get back to the tent and rest.

16:00. I prepared another dehydrated camping meal, but this one I had to force down. It did not taste good, but I knew I had no other option; I had to take in the calories. I lay down and tried to get more rest, but I could not sleep.

19:00. We were all in our sleeping bags trying to rest; I took out the Road Book to see what the following day had in store for us. Beatrice asked if I would read it to her, and this became one of the highlights in our tent that week because we were laughing so hard we were reduced to tears. We were all absolutely exhausted, well beyond being completely overtired, and the Road Book described how the following day would be full of sand. Again. By that point, after having endured nearly a week slogging through deep sand, we knew what that entailed. The description

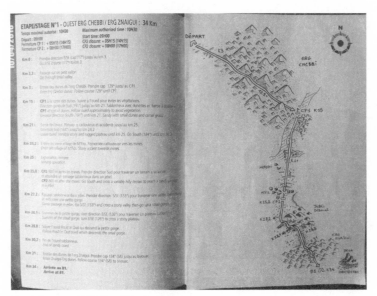

The infamous MdS Road Book

of the next day sounded so impossible, as if it couldn't be true, really at the point of being ridiculous. It read like a comedy act, though it was full of simple facts. Obviously, I threw in a lot of sarcasm as I read and modified the text slightly with my giddiness, "Enter dunes, go 3.1 kilometers. Exit dunes. Reenter dunes, go 5 kilometers." "Deceptive, variably stony rise." Seriously, it said that. We couldn't fathom what that possible could mean. Deceptive? Would there be monstrous sand dunes hidden behind the stony rise? "Sandy hill to the left. Enter dunes. Exit dunes. Small sparse dunes with camel grass." Where were we supposed to be able to run? Beatrice said the book was hilarious, but I told her it was simply "well written."

20:00. We laughed ourselves to sleep.

CHAPTER 16

MY FIRST ULTRA

The first entry in my diary for that 84.3-kilometer stage of the Marathon des Sables, which had taken me over 19 hours to complete, read "that was the most physically and mentally strenuous day of my life." Obviously being able to run races like that doesn't happen overnight, and unless you are Dean Karnazes, you don't just wake up one day and run 30 miles without any training.

Sports have always been an important part of my life since I was very young. The Red Sox, Celtics, and Patriots were regulars on our television. I played team sports in school, including soccer, softball, basketball, and field hockey, and I even ran cross-country in junior high (but hated it!). In college I played field hockey and lacrosse. Through all those years, even during all four of my pregnancies, I ran regularly to stay in shape. Saying I "ran regularly" needs to be put into perspective because at that time it was actually what most "normal" people do—two to three times per week for about 45 minutes. It wasn't until after the birth of my fourth child that I took part in a local race, a 5K. My goal was simply to run it under 30 minutes. I ran it in 27, and, absolutely thrilled, I subsequently became addicted to racing. I bought a GPS watch and watched how my distances got longer and my speed increased. I can still remember the feeling of absolute euphoria the first time I ran 10 kilometers. I began taking part in 10K races, so the eventual jump to longer distances was a natural transition. My first marathon was four years after that initial 5K race, and a year after that I ran my first ultra.

Why are some people perfectly happy with their 5- or 10-kilometer races and others crave the long distances? My motivation had a lot to do with a book: *Ultramarathon Man* by Dean Karnazes (with this book title a respectful homage to his). The man is a phenomenon and takes on adventure with so much enthusiasm that it is hard not to be caught up in the excitement. Most people of course won't do it—run an ultra, that is—but I knew after I read his book that it was only a matter of time before I attempted my first one.

True to form, that time came sooner than expected.

The Amberger Ultramarathon, which is a charity event that takes place annually at the beginning of November, is a "group" race, meaning it is noncompetitive. It is run at a 6:00 minute per kilometer pace (about 9.5 min/ mile), and runners can choose their distance at 10-kilometer intervals, so they run anywhere

With Dean Karnazes at the 2013 Boston Marathon Expo

between 10 kilometers and the entire length of the course, which is just over 63 kilometers (nearly 40 miles). There are refreshment stations approximately every 10 kilometers where runners can enter or leave courtesy of a shuttlebus and where the group takes a short 3- to 4-minute break to rc-nourish before continuing together when a whistle is blown. Over 200 runners participate, with about 80 completing the entire course. I had learned about the race via the Armin Wolf Laufteam Newsletter as it was one of the team's scheduled events. Being one of the newer members of the team, I felt I should try to take part in that race, if possible. Since I'd been training to run the Berlin Marathon at the end of September, I would have the perfect training preparation for my first ultra. Although I hadn't planned on running an ultra quite yet, the group format appealed to me, and I thought, why not? But life loves to throw us curve balls.

During a race in the middle of September, I was injured and then "sidelined" due to inflammation on my ischium, which caused considerable sciatica pain. I tried intensive physical therapy and other home remedies to get me back in shape, but three days before the marathon in Berlin I knew it wasn't going to happen, and I canceled my trip.

The next question was obviously, what about Amberg? I knew it was not likely that I'd be able to complete more than part of the ultra. Although I had begun training again, it was minimal. Then two weeks before Amberg I found myself back at the orthopedist in considerable pain and begging for help. He said, "It takes time." I told him that I wanted to run an ultramarathon in two weeks. He laughed and told me, "Well then, the pain level hasn't reached your limits yet." I left the office limping, feeling dejected, and hoping for a miracle.

A week later that miracle happened. I woke up one morning pain free (P.S. Thanks, God).

So, there I was, a week before my first ultra, having had only one training run over 30 kilometers in more than two months and banking everything on successive days of mid- to mid-long runs to avoid reinjury (four days whereby I run 25-30 kilometers on one day, about 15 the next, then 18-20, then 10-15 before a day off). Not to mention that I was very scared but super excited!

Taper, taper, taper. Rest. And before I knew it, the day had arrived. Runners from the Armin Wolf Team met at 7am in Regensburg, and we drove the hour up to Amberg together in a van. Most of the other team members planned to run 10 to 30 kilometers, but one other planned to run the full distance. I had previously told Armin (our team's namesake) that I would plan to run just the marathon distance, and, still worried about the injury, I would see how I felt about continuing on with the ultra after 42 kilometers. Armin must have misunderstood (or knows me too well) and announced to the team when we met that morning that I was going to run the full distance (oh, boy, let's not talk about pressure).

We arrived at 8:15 in Amberg for a 9am start, but there was no one there except for us. Not even the organizers. And it was cold. Just over freezing, though temps were supposed to get to about 8 degrees Celsius (46 °F) that day. Shortly thereafter someone arrived and let us into the school which was the start/finish. Inside we were given our starting numbers, which were simply the number of kilometers that we planned to run. My start number was: 63. Ugh.

Five minutes before the start we gathered in front of the school. There were about one hundred of us, and a local priest blessed the race and the runners. Godspeed was definitely what I'd need.

Then, rather unceremoniously, we were off. The first ten kilometers were easy and fun; there were a lot of us from the running team, and all were full of energy. The tempo was upbeat, and everyone was chatting. I noticed the smell of fabric softener in the air and commented that in a few hours that odor would be gone from the sportswear and replaced with one much less pleasant.

At kilometer 11.5 we came into the first rest station, drank some hot tea, said goodbye to most of our teammates, then the remaining few of us were off again when the whistle blew after a couple of minutes. The spirit was still great, and the weather was holding, which is to say it did not rain, though it was heavily overcast. I recall that at about kilometer 20, I saw the road go off in the distance into what seemed like oblivion...it appeared endless and then crescendoed over a substantial hill. I began to have doubts. *I don't want to run that far* is what I thought. The distance before me was probably only 2 kilometers and not the 40-plus that I still had to run. This was going to be a challenge.

The second rest station was again a farewell to several teammates and, after another quick drink of hot tea and a piece of banana, we were on our way again. Soon after, we ran through some very muddy tractor paths full of puddles. Some runners thought it was funny to run straight through and splash the rest of us. Considering that I had several hours in front of me, the thought of wet feet and clothes at those chilly temps was not appealing, and I tried to steer clear of those jovial boys.

Kilometer 25 brought another surprise—a flooded field! The path was covered in water, so everyone dispersed along the edges of the field, but it was still very wet there. We just couldn't find a dry path. Runners were scattered everywhere. Where there were not puddles, the ground was extremely soft, daring us to try to stay on top and not sink down into its squishiness. That was slow-going; it took quite a bit of concentration and energy, but it was also pretty entertaining.

I was then looking forward to the next rest stop at kilometer 30 where my husband, Frank, and two of our kids, Robert and Amelia, would be waiting. They would also have some fresh clothes for me to change into. It was good to see them, and Amelia was my little helper who gave me a clean shirt and jacket and also asked what else I might need (well trained). More energy gels? At this rest stop, I filled my bottles with tea, ate another piece of banana, drank some water, and said goodbye to the last from our team other than Armin (a different one, not the team's namesake) who was also running the entire distance. Armin is an extremely experienced ultrarunner, with over 70 of them to his credit. It was a solace to know that he would be there to help me along. So, from that point on, we ran the last 30-plus kilometers together.

The following twelve kilometers brought us first through some rolling hills and forest and then into the outskirts of the city of Amberg. It was in the city that the next rest station was located and that was at the classic marathon mark, kilometer 42. The milestone didn't register with me at first until Armin made the comment that our marathon time wasn't so great. I then looked at my watch and saw that we had reached the point in 4 hours and 15 minutes. Ok, if we had been running on flat, paved roads... sure, but considering what we'd just traversed, I thought the time was pretty impressive! At that stop, I drank some Coke, ate a piece of banana, refilled the tea in my bottles, and hung on my husband's shoulder (sitting was not an option) before the whistle blew, and we were off again.

I was rejuvenated at this point because I knew that every step I now made took me farther than I'd ever run before (or maybe it was the Coke). Since we were past the marathon mark, I was now officially running an ultra, regardless of how far I'd eventually make it.

The next milestone for me was the 50-kilometer point, and I was thrilled when my watch beeped to mark it. But right after that I experienced a major low point. A headwind picked up, there was a long incline in front of us, and I still had 14 kilometers to go. I wanted to cry. At this point, conversation in the group was reduced to null. Everyone was fighting their own internal battles, and I simply tried to concentrate on good technique. One foot in front of the other.

Kilometer 52 was the last checkpoint, and Armin was considering stopping. I told him, "No way are you leaving me now, this close to the end!" It didn't take any more coaxing to get him going. He got right up from the fence he was leaning against and ran with me as the whistle blew for the last time.

Those final kilometers were a struggle. I kept thinking that I had a multitude of muscle aches, but when I took an objective evaluation, I was actually in good shape, so I tried to concentrate instead on the beautiful surroundings and imagine that I was just on a 10K fun-run with some friends. Again, I had to fight back tears at one point. But at no moment did I consider stopping.

Back into a thickly wooded trail, a runner next to me suddenly had severe cramps in his hamstring. No one had magnesium tablets with them, but I had a small salt packet which I gave him along with one of my water bottles. We were only about five kilometers from the finish, and he kept limping along, accompanied by the race sweeper (race organizer who stayed in the back throughout the entire race).

The sun started to sink in the sky as we came out of the woods and onto paved roads for the last 3-kilometer stretch. We passed through a small village, but there were no spectators to cheer us on. We ran in silence, simply going through the same physical motions that our bodies had been enduring for more than six hours. Then suddenly the school came into view, the same school we had arrived at that morning as the sun had just begun to appear over the horizon.

We'd spent the entire day running.

My two youngest kids came sprinting toward me and joined me over the last hundred meters. I was overwhelmed with the feeling of accomplishment. I'd done it. There was no official finish line, no finish time, no spectators. Just the group of runners being greeted and congratulated by their families. I waited outside for the last runner, the man with the cramps, and by this time he was back to running again. He thanked me as he returned my water bottle and said the cramps were gone.

Everyone then filed into the school to get some hot coffee and sugary cakes. I drank a cup of coffee and sat down for a few minutes. I probably could have run farther had I not stopped, but after sitting down, my body gave up on me. My eight-year-old daughter had to lead me into the locker room, help me undress, and guide me into the shower. Any movement the rest of the day was painful. Climbing stairs was nearly impossible. I was very tired. After a good dinner I was in bed at 8pm and slept 12 hours. I got up the next morning feeling pretty good, but then by 1pm I was so kaput that I had to lie down and sleep for another two hours! Following dinner, I was again in bed at 7:30 that second night, and after another 11 hours of sleep, I was back to my old self. A few muscle aches, but nothing significant, and by the third day I was ready to run again.

But, well, I didn't. I took a full eight days off, as hard as it was. And during that time, I began scouring the Internet, looking for my next ultra.

CHAPTER 17

MDS STAGE 5

HASSI TARFA TO BOU MAKHLOUF, 42.2 KM

7:00. An early start today! The MdS offered a program for runners' families to come watch the last leg of the race and also to walk together with us as part of the UNICEF Charity stage the next day. So there were some families at the start of the race, giving it a completely different feel, as if it were a race back home. It was nice. After the start the family members were then shuttled back and forth to the checkpoints via quad vehicles so that they could see the race in progress.

I felt really strong from the start. The day of rest had done me good, but it was too early to tell if and when I would break in. The leg was 42.2 kilometers (26 miles), a full marathon, so there was no telling what could happen during that time. Another sandstorm? Rocky climbs? *Deceptive* sandy dunes? I ran for some time at the beginning with Friso from the Netherlands, who I had crossed paths with many times during the week, most notably when he saw me in dire straits at CP5 on the long stage. He was pushing it, trying to break into the top 300 for the overall end ranking. He kept saying that we were making good time and that we were contending for place 299, but at the time I really wasn't concerned about which place I ended up in; I knew that the long stage had severely hurt my ranking, and I just wanted to finish the day—because it was the last official run, and then I would be a MdS Finisher!

8:30. Arriving at checkpoint 1, I still felt good. The early start also meant it was cooler and easier to run.

As is tradition in the race, on this last day, the 100 best ranked runners start 1.5 hours later, so they were just starting as I was arriving at CP1. The cool thing about this was that I was essentially in the lead group, or at least I could keep them in eye's reach, and I was one of the first women to enter the checkpoints. There were also several family members there at CP1, and whether they knew about the second start or not, I was one of the first women that they saw, so there were lots of cheers for me. It was wonderful; I felt like they were my own family. It motivated me to make as short a stop as possible and to keep pushing on to see what I could achieve. But first I had to take care of business: fill my water bottles and take my salt tablets. As I pulled out my packet of salt tablets from my pouch, Friso, who was standing next to me, mentioned that he had lost his and asked if he could have one of mine. One, of course, would be ridiculous. He'd need about 10 for the stage alone, and since we were provided with about 100 tables, almost twice what I'd need myself, I poured a small pile out into his hand. To this he responded with a big smile, "I love you."

Running stage 5 of the MdS
© MARATHON DES SABLES 2016

We took off from CP1, and I slowly lost sight of Friso, who ended up finishing 15 minutes before me and took the 289th place in the overall end ranking, and funnily enough I landed in spot 299! We laughed about this at the awards ceremony later that night.

10:00. Checkpoint 2 at kilometer 24.2. Here I saw Elisabeth from the Netherlands. Just as I was arriving, she was leaving.

11:15. Female leader, Natalia Sedykh, who had started 1.5 hours after me, finally passed me at kilometer 32. I heard someone coming up from behind and was surprised to hear a woman's voice cheering me on saying, "Go, Holly! Go, Go, Go!" At the time we were in some small sandy dunes, and I had just begun walking, but as she passed by me at a run, I thought, hey, if she can run, so can I! So I began running again, albeit not at her pace, but

I never stopped after that, except briefly for water at the last checkpoint, until I crossed the finish line!

11:30. Checkpoint 3 at kilometer 34.2. I arrived here at the same time as Elisabeth, and as we filled our water bottles, took our salt, and had a couple of bites to eat she asked me if we could run together for a while. Great! Of course, it makes it more enjoyable to share the adventure and the time goes by faster. But, her pace was a little faster than mine, and it was more of an effort for me. I kept with her, though, and after a few kilometers she said she needed to stop and walk a bit. I told her that I had to keep running, albeit a little slower, and that we'd see each other later. For me it is much easier to stay in a running motion rather than to disrupt my rhythm by a walk–run approach, but everyone is different. Those last several kilometers were amazing. I could see the finish line from a long distance away, and though it is frustrating because it just never seems to get any closer, I gave it all I had. The ground was hard and flat, so I just had to concentrate on one foot in front of the other.

12:30. When I crossed the finish line it felt as though I had been running for no time at all. I guess even 42.2 kilometers can be short in the larger scheme of things. It seemed like everyone who'd just finished was still standing there cheering on each and every runner that came in. The crowd just kept getting bigger as so many familiar names and faces from the week kept coming into view.

One of the family members waiting for a finisher asked me about how long it took to get from CP3 to the finish. I answered that it took me 55 minutes, and two guys standing next to me exclaimed,

I just officially finished the 31st Marathon des Sables
© MARATHON DES SABLES 2016

"Wow! You were fast!" Ironically, though, when you get to the point of considering covering 8 kilometers in 55 minutes to be fast, you can understand the extremity of this race. I stayed there for about half an hour before going to the tent to drop off my stuff, but returned for about another hour to watch the joy on the people's faces as they finished.

17:00.   I was hungry. I didn't have any more camping meals for that day, and the thought of just another couple of sports bars for the evening was depressing. Beatrice picked up on this. She had two extra camping meals after being a guest of the "lovely British woman" on the long stage, but both of her meals contained meat, so she went on a hunt for me. A few minutes later she returned and had traded her goulash for dehydrated pasta with vegetables! Yippee! I was going to eat like a queen tonight!

18:30. We were just about to start a fire for our meals when we were told by the organization that the awards ceremony would be at 19:00, so we decided to wait until after the formality to eat. This had been a poor decision, as we realized later, because the ceremony lasted longer than we thought.

19:00. Awards ceremony. We were weak, hungry, and thirsty. We had brought no water with us, since we thought it would be short. We seemed to always be in a borderline state of dehydration, and most people were seen with bottles of water in their hand no matter where they went. We were all in the same boat: Everyone looked like zombies, and most of us were sitting on the dusty ground during the ceremony simply because we didn't have the strength to remain standing without even having something to lean on. Beatrice and I were lucky, though, to have gotten a spot next to the large blow-up gate of the finish line, and we sort of leaned or sat on that, though the air kept redistributing itself when anyone moved, and we'd find ourselves falling into each other or getting catapulted onto the ground.

20:00. Finally had time to cook something to eat. The guys started a fire and thankfully gave me some of their boiling water once Cap was given his meal. I was starving and feeling very weak. The pasta and veggie dish was one of the most amazing meals I've ever eaten.

That night the winds were ferocious, worse than they had been all week. The guys had dropped down the back "wall" of the tent, but it wasn't very stable. It was flapping around, and there was still a gap. Unfortunately for me, lying in the middle of the tent, this gap was right behind my head, but the walls on both sides of the tent were collapsed so far down that there was nowhere else for me to go. I was lying in the middle of a wind tunnel that was pummeling dust and dirt and shrub brush all over me and anything else in its path. I couldn't sleep, but I also knew that alone I wouldn't be able to fix the tent; the poles were too heavy, and the wind was too strong. I just huddled down as deep as I could in my sleeping bag and curled up to retain as much of my own body heat as possible. It was going to be my last night out in the desert, and I knew I'd survive it.

CHAPTER 18

RUNNING FROM WILD GAME

Even when I'm not out running in foreign environments such as the desert, sometimes I find myself having some really wild adventures upon going out for what I'd thought would be seemingly uneventful training runs.

One such adventure happened on our first day of vacation in Mallorca, when I couldn't wait to get out on the trails. I woke early and tip-toed around in the dark, trying not to wake my husband and young son as I got into my running clothes (which I'd laid out the night before), grabbed my gear, and snuck out the door.

We were staying on the Formentor peninsula in the northeast of Mallorca. Our hotel was on the water and just behind it was a huge granite outcropping. I wanted to run to the top of that. So the evening before I asked at reception about trails in the area and was given a hand-sketched map with vague instructions about having to run around the outcropping and then up from the backside. It would have to do. I mean, I was on a peninsula which is no more than a few kilometers across at its widest. How could I get lost?

…Though now I'm beginning to think I could get lost in my own closet. But I digress…

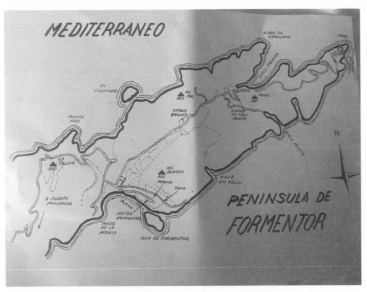

Map of the Formentor peninsula

I headed out, full of high hopes, but what should have taken me about 10 minutes to get to the trailhead actually took me 30. *In the back of the large parking lot at the bottom of the street,* the hotel receptionist told me, but she wasn't very specific about which large parking lot it was, and upon driving in the day before my attention was not drawn to the local parking lot varieties. *You'll then have to climb over a fence,* she told me, *there are signs that say Private Property, but don't worry, we own the property.* So the first parking lot I entered had a rough trail that ended up on a road, which I crossed over onto a fire road which indeed led to a relatively high chain-link fence with barbed wire on the top but no Private Property sign. Hmm....what to do? Of course I scaled the fence and kept on running, but as the fire road turned to a trail which eventually disappeared, I found myself on a steep incline picking through yucca plants, prickly bushes, and climbing stone walls on all fours (making as much noise as possible to ward off snakes); I soon realized that I was way off. So I backtracked, cutting myself twice rescaling the fence, and not too long afterward I found the correct parking lot which had a sturdy A-frame ladder built over a hiker-friendly fence. I was on my way!

About a kilometer later I was faced with my next major decision. A branch of the main trail turned off toward the direction of

Warning sign

the outcropping I wanted to climb, so I turned onto it and was immediately faced with a large sign warning me of wild game in the area. What kind of wild game? It didn't say. I was going through options in my head. Snakes? Wild boar? Bears? So, to be prudent, which I normally am not, I stayed on the main trail, which then meandered past a farm which had a huge herd of sheep, most adorned with bells around their necks, like cows in the Alps. So, for a short time I ran along enjoying the scenery until I came across another trail branch also in the direction I wanted to head, which did not have a posted warning sign. Yippee!

And then I came across a dead sheep. And then another. And another. And then a huge pile of sheep bones in a dried-out creek bed...with a freshly dead sheep laying on top. Not yippee.

Pile of bones and a recently deceased sheep

I kept moving upward toward my goal, and the trail got narrower and narrower. Suddenly, there was a big, black goat standing on a rock above me. By the time I got my camera out, he was gone. I moved on but was having trouble keeping track of the trail…was it there? Or there? Did I miss something? Then more goats. I was now simply breaking through scrub brush, scaling large rocks, wishing I'd worn long socks, and slowly coming to the realization that any semblance of a trail I came across had nothing to do with human traversal, but rather that of goats.

In the company of goats

After an hour and a half since leaving the hotel, with the mountain peak in view (yes, by now it is a mountain, not an outcropping), I got caught in a spider web. I mean really caught. This thing was massively sticky and strong. I quickly tried to back away and squirmed around to get free of the strands, all the time praying that the homeowner would not show up to retrieve its prey (a.k.a., me).

I pushed on and when I finally ended up on a plateau I began to have some hope of reaching my desired destination, so I simply found the best goat trails and headed for the highest point. Then suddenly the path dumped me out onto a very well-maintained dirt road! What? Where did that come from? How did that get up here and why did I not come up on that? Ugh.

I followed the road until it ended and then continued on a well-worn, single-track trail. Pyramids of small rocks were also built at random points along the way to help mark the path, which otherwise would have been easy to lose track of when it crossed over large flat rock. After another 20 minutes or so, I finally reached the top (of something). I wasn't really sure where I was, if it was indeed the rocky outcropping above my hotel or somewhere else, so I began slowly edging down the other side and finally was rewarded with a magnificent view of the bay in front of our hotel. However, I couldn't find any access to get down from that side. I could even see the hotel tennis courts below, but there was a severe drop-off, so I decided to play it safe and go back down along the dirt road that I had found before.

Sounds like the end of the story, right? Think again.

The road seemed to be laughing at me as I easily jogged down and eventually passed by where I had fatefully turned off the main

View from the mountaintop

trail two hours before. I was getting tired and looking forward to breakfast.

Just as I began to see the light at the end of the tunnel, something jumped out of the bushes at me and let out a terrible shriek! From pure instinct I immediately began to sprint, but the creature was right on my heels, still with a constant, high-pitched screaming!

Without slowing down I turned around to see what kind of monster was hoping to have me for breakfast, and I was startled to find…a baby lamb was chasing me.

Ok, don't laugh. This was serious. I have encountered snakes, moose, wild boar, and even had a buzzard scrape its talons over my scalp, but I have never before been so scared of an animal as I was of this tiny creature. It had probably been separated from its family and was hoping I could help, but something in its behavior and the way it was yelping sent alarm signals. The thought of rabies crossed my mind. I'll bet you didn't know that baby sheep can run fast. Really fast. After 100 meters all-out, the animal was still right behind me and still screaming. I kept up the pace and even after another 100 meters it was still there! I knew if I stopped it would jump on me. What would I do? Throw rocks? I didn't want to risk slowing down, so I kept it up until finally, after about 400 meters (a quarter mile), it gave up. *Whew.*

The velocity spike on my GPS data is impossible to miss.

Relaying my story on the hotel veranda

Ten minutes later I was finally back at the hotel, and after a quick shower, I met my family for breakfast, showed them my legs which were scratched from ankle to hip, and told them about my adventure and frightful encounter with Mallorca's Wild Game. Why was I the only one not laughing?

I ran the beginning of that same trail the following morning, albeit with my hubby along for "protection," and there on the side of the trail we saw the lamb again, but today he wasn't screaming. Today he lay dead. My husband said my instinct was probably right and that the sheep may have been sick, but I still couldn't help but feel a pang of guilt.

Like I said, baby sheep aren't the only animals I've been chased after while running. Other incredible animal encounters I've

Having fun with the kids (with the "mountain" outcropping in the background)

experienced include coming face-to-face with a moose in the wilds of northern Sweden, as well as being confronted by a mother wild boar who had a pack of squeakers (really, that's what baby boars are called). That incident sent me climbing up a chain-link fence until Mother Boar decided to go back to her business of foraging rather than scaring the hell out of me.

Several times I'd become the intended prey to a couple of our local buzzards. Usually I would be running along the edges of some fields adjacent to tall trees, minding my own business, when I would hear the bird's angry call. Then it would circle above me and dive down back and forth several times in an attempt to scare me away. Usually yelling and waving my arms scares them off, and I'm on my way again.

But there were two attacks that bordered on scary. (Ok, they were scary.) The first one happened when I was running through a field in a huge stretch of farmland interspersed with rows of tall trees and patches of woods. I heard the bird's scream, and it came at me very low five or six times and followed me for a couple hundred meters. This bird was huge; it almost looked like an owl, but a scary mean owl, not Hedwig. I was actually lost at the time, so fleeing for my life on top of that was not what I had planned for an easy Sunday morning run.

The second attack only three days later and about 20 kilometers away was different. I didn't see or hear the bird beforehand. Then suddenly I heard a *whooshhhh* and felt something lightly touch the top of my head! I looked up to see this massive bird right in front of me! It flew up, turned around, and came right back at me. I began screaming and waving my arms. It wasn't impressed with my antics and just kept circling and diving down toward me.

Finally this feathered fiend flew back into its tree, and I started running again. But 30 seconds or so later I turned back around just to be sure that it was truly gone, and the beast was about 10 meters away, like a kamikaze pilot zeroing in on me at high speed! He had that angry bird look, and I screamed and began waving my arms around as much as I could. At that point I just kept running, constantly turning around to keep the bird in sight, which continued to circle, until I was finally far enough away to be out of its territory, I guess.

I was a bit dumbfounded by this whole scenario. Maybe it had babies in a nest nearby? Does my strawberry-blond ponytail look like a fox tail?

When I got home and told my family about the latest attack, my middle daughter, Sophie, became worried. She did some research on the Internet about why it happens and what to do if it does. My favorite part of her research: "They attack because you are fast and dangerous."

Clearly birds are very intelligent creatures.

CHAPTER 19

MDS UNICEF CHARITY STAGE

BOU MAKHLOUF TO OUR BUSES WAITING TO RETURN US TO CIVILIZATION, 17.7 KM

5:30. Woke with the camp and prepared last meal! Ok, nothing to prepare—the bars are ready to eat—but I was still overjoyed that our next meal would be a bag lunch in the bus, and finally a hot, cooked meal with fresh salad and vegetables in the hotel that night!

7:30. Collected water and fresh, clean shirts for the charity run! We were each given a blue cotton T-shirt which we were required to wear that day. It was nice to be in something clean, but the heavy cotton was not the best material for the desert, and it was soaked with sweat soon after the start. Although participation in the UNICEF charity run–walk was required by all MdS participants in order to be an official finisher of the entire race, the running times for the day were not added to the race total,

181

but rather were counted separately. So very few runners actually "raced" on that day. Most decided to walk the 17.7-kilometer (11 miles) route with their newfound friends or tentmates. Our Tent 40 planned the same.

8:30.   Start. Beatrice kept me entertained with her chatting. I felt exhausted. The heat was extraordinary, and walking was more strenuous on me than running, so Beatrice was critical in getting me through that day.

I kept my eyes to the ground and looked for fossils and 'dinosaur' bones for the kids, since I was finally able to put something in my backpack and carry it without worrying about having to schlep around any extra weight. I also found tons of seashells! Amazing what a million years can do to a landscape.

12:30.   Finish. Hot tea. Official photos. Then out to the rows of buses to find a SEAT in AIR CONDITIONING! Absolute heaven. As we got on the bus, we were given a bag lunch and some fresh bread. I could have cried with joy. The bus ride took nearly six hours, but no one complained. We were all rather quiet; some dozed, others just looked out the windows at what would be for some of us the last glimpses of the desert.

Shells and "dino" bones found during the charity stage

18:30. Shower! Internet! Beatrice and I were sharing a room, and we immediately began digging through our suitcases which had just been returned to us after giving them up a week earlier in the desert. We were checking to see what we had available for shampoo, soap, and conditioner. Beatrice was upset when she found her deodorant spray bottle didn't work, and then I found that I had a mini travel deo in my bag. We giggled like school girls and were the two happiest women on earth!

My hair after nine days without washing it

20:00. A beer! Incredible salad buffet! Fresh bread! The atmosphere in the restaurant was celebratory. Although I'd spent most of the week with these people, it was hard

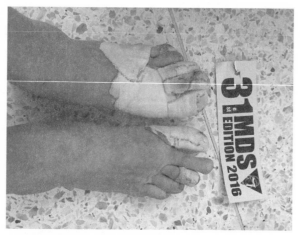

The wreck that were once my feet

to recognize many of them at first after they'd showered and were in casual clothes. Most of us were busy with the Internet, writing to family and friends, catching up on the news, or checking where we'd ended up in the rankings of the MdS. I placed 31st out of the women and 299th overall. I was a little bit disappointed with the women's ranking, which was entirely due to my results in the long stage, but you never know what can happen in ultras, and that's one of the mysteries of the sport that brings us back. It is a challenge for the mind as well as the body.

22:30. Got into a real bed for the first time in over a week for my last night in Morocco. I did not sleep well. I looked at my clock several times during the night, afraid I would miss my alarm. I didn't, of course. I woke on time and shared a taxi with three local men to the airport. My flight had a stopover in Madrid. The line to get through customs and enter the EU was insanely long. But after what I'd been through the week before, I felt stronger than anyone on earth, so I focused straight ahead, walked right past the line, ducked under some expandable guide rails, and headed straight for a customs window that had one person waiting. I was through in five minutes whereas had I waited in that line I would have missed my connection. I didn't care; I was a woman on a mission: Getting home.

Back in Munich I was greeted by my happily waiting family. They had a huge hand-painted sign, flowers, and a caricature of me in the desert. I was so overjoyed to be in the safety of their presence and knew that now I could relax and let down my guard for the first time in ten days. Our reunion also entertained the other passengers who were smiling ear to ear. Out in the car, a cooler of my beloved snacks was waiting for me, and at home there was enough of my favorite foods to feed an army. Two of our good friends came over that night to celebrate and hear my stories.

Homecoming at the Munich airport

But my feet hurt badly. They were swollen from the race and aggravated further by the flights. Standing and lying down were okay, but sitting was agony. One of our friends is also my physical therapist and he scheduled me to come into his office the next morning for lymphatic drainage therapy.

All in all, I was in great shape. No serious injuries, and although it would take me a while to work through the mental struggle of the long stage, what would be left were incredible memories to last a lifetime. When I think back on it, I realize it was an amazing adventure full of contrasts: It was both incredible and horrible. The highs were extremely high, and the lows exceedingly low. Sometimes I felt as though

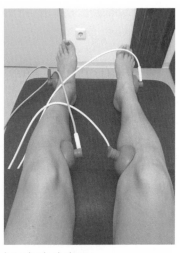
Lymphatic drainage

I were in an Arabian fairytale and then suddenly thrown into a nightmare. The challenge gave me so many positive elements but not without having me suffer dearly for them.

Above all, I am grateful and deeply impressed by the support and encouragement of the volunteers, media crew, and doctors. The entire staff was always positive, helpful, cheerful, informative, and caring. We runners came to love every one of those familiar faces as they greeted our weary bodies with a smile and encouragement while passing out bottles of water at each checkpoint or asking, "Ca va?" as we reached the top of a treacherous climb. Without them, achieving the mind-boggling would have been nearly impossible.

Our tentmates became an integral part in the overall sense of comfort and security, as well, because we shared a 12-square-meter space that served as home for nine days. A peaceful environment where each played a supportive role was critical to ease the discomforts of living an exceptionally rudimentary existence.

I found that the course distance was not the greatest obstacle, but rather the terrain and weather. Running the marathon distance on hard-packed soil is relatively easy and straight-forward for someone who is even mediocrely trained in endurance. But running the same distance over dunes where one is forced to walk with intense effort, or climbing rocky mountain passes where use of your hands is also essential, or battling fierce winds and sand beating against your body, well, that's another story.

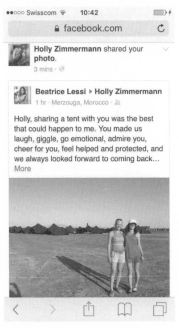

Message from Beatrice

There were officially 136 people who had to abandon the race, including Laurence Klein, the recent winner and woman who I'd overtaken in stage 2. Obviously something had been wrong then, which was pretty clear to me at the time simply by the fact that I was passing her!

I've been asked many times whether I will run the Marathon des Sables in Morocco again, and I don't have to waste a moment's thought on the answer.

No. Period. But it was an experience that I will always cherish.

That first night home, as I tucked my youngest daughter into bed, she looked up at me as if seeing me for the first time and said, "I'm so glad you're my mama."

And with those few words, everything had been worth it.

CHAPTER 20

RUNNING WITH FERRAGAMO

I met a lot of interesting people in Morocco—my tentmates, the other runners, the volunteers, the doctors, and the photographers. They came from over 40 countries all over the world to unite for an event which is almost unthinkable in its scope, not only for the runners who have the grueling course to battle, but also the logistics of providing safety and shelter for more than a thousand people in a hostile environment is an amazing feat in itself.

From all corners of the globe, people love running. From the barefoot Tarahumara in Mexico to some of our world leaders, it is a common thread in humanity that is not divided by language, culture, or environment. If you find a comfortable pace with someone, the conversation flows, regardless if it's your best friend or a complete stranger. Running unites us despite our differences.

A couple of years ago my oldest daughter, Juliana, and I visited my aunt Simonetta in Florence, Italy. Simonetta has spent decades working in the fashion industry for many well-known fashion

ULTRAMARATHON MOM

houses and, after living most of her life in New York, she was spending a couple of years in Florence and working with Roberto Cavalli. (When I say "with," that really means at his side, while also taking his own daughter under her tutorial wing and teaching her the tricks of the trade.)

For our stay in Florence, we had to get a hotel since Simonetta's niece from the other side of the family was staying at her place for a few months. But the hotel was only a few hundred meters away from her apartment. And the hotel, Villa la Vedetta, was absolutely fabulous! Gorgeous pool, terrace, and views over the city—perfect pampering for us girls!

As always when traveling, I wanted to make sure that I got in at least one decent run while there, so I asked my aunt if she had a friend who could run 15 to 20 kilometers with me, and her answer was, "The only person I know who runs those distances here is James Ferragamo." And she said she'd talk to him about it.

What can I say? There certainly are worse running partners out there.

Of course, I thought it would never happen, but anyone who knows my aunt Simonetta knows that once she puts her mind to something, it almost always comes to fruition. Guess it runs in the family. For those of you who are not familiar with the Ferragamo name, the next time you are in a major city, strolling through the luxury store district, next to Prada, Gucci, and Chanel, then be aware of that store with the beautifully crafted windows showcasing exquisite shoes, handbags, and clothes and above which in lovely script is written the name: Salvatore Ferragamo.

I have to admit, though, I wasn't really sure into which generation James fit into the family—an active octogenarian?

190

A 20-something-year-old? So I looked him up. And wouldn't you know, he is my age and (ahem) very attractive. He also just happened to be the director of women's leather products for the family business.

Shit. Now I'm nervous. I didn't search any more. I just wanted to go for a run with a *normal* person!

So, the next week, after I'd almost forgotten the whole thing (well, not really), Simonetta sends me James' personal cell phone number and said that he and I should work it out for ourselves. I immediately went to my teenage daughter, held out my phone, and announced that I was now in possession of his number. She squealed with delight, and the two of us plopped down together on the couch, giggling away, to check out his WhatsApp profile photo. I was almost afraid to touch anything on the phone for fear of mistakenly sending an audio byte, a goofy smiley, or pressing the call button. But with pinpoint precision I managed to save him into my contact list. *Whew.*

Now what? I'm not good at things like this. I HATE the telephone. I could possibly be the only woman on earth who despises talking on the phone, so calling him was not an option. I'd text him. Maybe. Ugh.

But I'd have to sleep on it first.

The next morning, Wednesday, Juliana and I left at 6am for Florence. The ride was long; longer than I thought. We arrived at our hotel at 2:30pm after combatting the curvy, narrow Brenner Pass and its brigade of trucks dominating the roads. Had I known what the drive entailed, we would have flown.

After checking into the hotel, I called my aunt to see what was planned…but she had broken her foot the day before and had to go to the hospital, so we wouldn't see her that night. Although, of course, she asked whether I had been in touch with James. Uh, no, I answered. Should I text him? Yes, she said…and mention you are my niece. (Duh.)

So, I texted him. Very unassuming…would be great if…yadda, yadda…something about not wanting to get lost running in Florence…blah, blah, blah…very flexible with the time….

An hour later came the reply…super relaxed… nice to meet you…Friday at 7pm would work for him.

I mean, Friday at 2 in the morning would have been ok for me. Really, now, who are we kidding here?

A couple of texts back and forth, and things were confirmed: he was to ~~pick me up~~ meet me at my hotel Friday at 7pm for our ~~evening out on the town~~ run. Ok, ok…I'm just a girl; let me romanticize things a bit! But since I didn't know the city and there was parking at my hotel it was really the easiest option for him to leave his car there.

Juliana asked, "Do you think he will come in a Ferrari?" One can only hope.

The next night, Thursday, we had dinner at my aunt's, and she told me that James had run the NYC marathon the year before. So, later, at my hotel, I checked the online results and was relieved to find out that his marathon times were about a half hour slower than mine. What? It's public info! I was afraid that the guy would run circles around me, and it was reassuring to know that I wouldn't have to struggle to keep up with him. I'm only human! Geez.

Friday was a great day. Slept late. Leisurely breakfast. Beautiful sunshine. A stroll through the gardens of the Palazzo Pitti followed by a bit more shopping, a late lunch, and then a couple of hours of relaxation at the pool. Well, Juliana was relaxed. I was not.

Oh, I have to mention, while shopping the day before, we stumbled upon the Salvatore Ferragamo fragrances in a perfumery and, after picking out a heavenly scent, Juliana said I had to buy it. I said that I would buy it after my run with him. Her don't-be-ridiculous look was all I needed to change my mind. So of course we decided I'd wear the scent while running with him and see if he recognizes it! He didn't. Or at least, he didn't mention it. Or maybe the smell of my sweat overpowered it?

At 10 minutes before 7, Juliana and I went down to the hotel gardens to wait. I checked the small parking lot, and there was a space available for him.

And, very punctual, at 7:01, he arrived. A nice car, but no Ferrari. I waved him into the back lot, and as soon as I saw him I knew this was going to be fun. He had a very easy manner, a friendly smile, and anyone in green, knee-length compression socks can't possibly be intimidating!

After some small talk with Juliana, we were on our way. I let him take the lead with the tempo which started out at a 5 min/km pace uphill. Oh, boy!

The tempo remained high, and the conversation flowed effortlessly—running, triathlons, family—but I avoided asking anything about his business since the main reason we were both out there was stress reduction.

At one point, as we were cruising along on a sidewalk, he suddenly took a sharp right turn and darted up a small set of stairs into a park. I had to stop and backtrack. "Hey, you need to put your turn signal on earlier!" I yelled to him. He laughed, and when I caught up to him, I added, "You don't have too many running partners, do you?" Another smile, and he shook his head, no.

We ran out of the city and up along the River Arno westward for several kilometers before crossing a bridge and returning on the other side. It was about 8:30pm by the time we reentered the city, and it was filling up for Friday night. We ran past Harry's Bar, every outdoor table occupied, where James said "…if you want to get a drink." Now? I asked. Another laugh and a headshake.

Then I almost got hit by a bus.

I was one step ahead of him as we entered a crosswalk. We both saw the bus coming from the left that was wanting to turn right across our path. James slammed on the brakes, but I kept going, certain that the bus would stop, or at least slow down, but it didn't. It did honk though…as if I didn't see this 10-ton colossus homing in on me! Needless to say, I narrowly made it by without getting nipped. I stopped on the other side, and after the bus passed between us, I saw the shocked look on James' face. He crossed over to me and said, "That was close." I told him my aunt would kill him if he let me get hit by a bus! That lightened the mood again, but I was pretty shaken.

We stayed along the river through the bustling city. James pointed out his store as we ran by. Then his restaurant. Restaurants now, too? Of course. Past the Ponte Vecchio and at one bridge farther downstream we crossed back over the river again.

Then, after 17.5 kilometers, the bottom of the last steep hill up to my hotel marked the end of our run as James stopped suddenly and announced, "I'm done." So we walked the last few hundred meters, holding hands. Just kidding!

Back at the hotel, some easy jokes, a sportsman's hand grip, and a couple of big smiles ended our session and the farewell.

I rushed upstairs to give Juliana the goods. After a shower and change, just as we were ready to head out the door to go have dinner with my aunt, I got a message on my cell phone. It was James, thanking me for the run and the company.

So I did get in a decent run with a *normal* person after all.

CHAPTER 21

100 KILOMETERS THROUGH THE NIGHT

When I got home from the Marathon des Sables, I was often confronted with the question of "What next?" I didn't really know myself how I could possibly top that adventure, but it had been so exciting that I began to search the Internet for my next special event. I couldn't find anything that really inspired me, except for one, the Polar Circle Marathon, which I had come across before. But the race for that year, scheduled at the end of October, was already full. So I put my name on the waiting list and focused on the other races that were already on my calendar.

I had several things that were already laid out and just eight weeks after returning from Morocco I was planning to run my first 100-kilometer event. My choice was the 100km Biel in Switzerland, and that race was also to serve as the culmination to a charity project which I "ran" with my friend, Tom, who'd I'd met at the trail running camp in the Swiss Alps that previous summer and met up with again at the Transviamala/ Transruinaulta in the fall. Back then he was thinking about organizing a charity project to help the massive numbers of refugees who were flooding into Europe. He knew from our conversations that, in addition to also being a running addict, I was moved by the plight of the refugees in Europe, and he thought I'd complement his project perfectly. He was right.

We named the endeavor Run4Refugees, decided on the format, and got underway promoting it on social media. We found sponsors to donate a chosen amount for every kilometer that we ran from January 1 until the finish line of the 100km Biel race. Tom's donations would go to the organization *Save the Children* in Switzerland while mine were focused on the Sindbad home of the Thomas-Wiser-Haus in Regensburg, Germany. Sindbad was a group home for young male refugees, all under 18 years of age, who, for various (and sometimes horrific) reasons, were in Germany without their parents or another legal guardian. (I use the past tense since the home is no longer used for that purpose since there are thankfully fewer refugees in need of that kind of care.)

I'd known about the Thomas-Wiser-Haus for a long time through its remedial education programs and shelters for children and young mothers. But through my running team, I was given the opportunity to visit their youth home for refugees. I was hesitant, not the least to say nervous, about visiting the home the first time. The residents at the time were 11 teenage boys from Africa and the Middle East, and due to the fact that Americans are sometimes not seen in the best light in the Middle East, I was not sure how they would react to me.

I went to visit the home with two other runners from the team along with our team founder and his wife. We brought with us food donations as well as some sporting goods, including two new soccer balls (all from private donors). We arrived in the late afternoon, and the agenda consisted of "sport," which would ideally be a game of soccer or running, and then dinner with the group.

Upon arrival we were greeted by the supervisor who was thrilled to have us there. She introduced us to a couple of the residents. A few of the boys were milling around, a couple of them sat in the community room on computers, and one boy was on a couch reading a book. A moment later another boy came out of the kitchen with a loaf of bread in his hand. A few brief words from the supervisor about not eating between meals, and the bread was quickly returned to the kitchen. I was impressed. The supervisor was stern yet understanding; the boy respectful. And this was to be a recurring theme of the evening. The boys were shy at first. They were hesitant about coming out and playing soccer with us. I mean, I don't blame them...I am a 40-something-year-old woman and the other two on the team included another woman (23 years old) and a young man (also 23). But eventually six of them came out with us to the field. Some had to remain at the home to prepare dinner. Each of them was required to contribute to the work in the home and had a rotational chore schedule which included cooking and cleaning.

Although I'd played soccer for years as a kid, it had been an eternity since I'd kicked the ball around. But, old habits die hard, and I quickly got my head and "skills" into the game. Some of the guys were good players and all showed great sportsmanship. It was muddy and slippery, and the play took on a great spirit.

Then, more than 30 minutes into the game, the impossible happened—I scored a header. It was a beautiful looping pass across the goal, and I instinctively jumped up and headed it above the keeper and into the net! My teammates exuberantly ran up to me with high fives, hooting and hollering. I was thrilled (and pretty impressed with myself). And even as the play resumed, some of the guys were in hysterical jubilation. I asked one of them why he was laughing so hard, and he answered, "Your header…it was just like on TV!"

Needless to say, the ice was broken, the roots of friendship began to take form, and my nervous anticipation of the evening was washed away.

After showering and convening at the dinner table, I sat next to one of the boys that I'd played ball with. His family was originally from Afghanistan but had lived for many years in Tehran, Iran. Although no one had introduced me as an American, and I had not volunteered the information, this one boy had heard my accent and knew it. I reluctantly asked him what he thought of America and Americans…and, thankfully, he was supportive of us. He was 16 years old, had only been in Germany for five months, and during that time, while living in the youth home, he had daily German lessons, as required of all residents, which enabled us to communicate exclusively in German. He could speak English quite well, but didn't want to use it. He wanted to practice the language of his new country, and we had absolutely no trouble understanding one another.

After some laughs and general conversation, I eventually got around to asking him how he'd come to Germany. On a boat? In a truck? He looked at me with a blank stare and answered: "No, I walked."

I was briefly speechless. You walked? From Tehran to Munich? "Yes," he answered. (I've since looked this up, and it is over

4,000 kilometers/2,500 miles). And how long did it take you? "About one month," he replied. Then he explained that his father had saved up money and hired a guided group. There were ten in the troop, and they would walk for hours or days on end before being lucky enough to be given a ride in a truck for a couple of hours before they were set back out on their feet. What about sleep? I asked. "Not much," he answered.

Then the story really began to make an impact as he told me that once he was in Germany and contacted his worried family back in Tehran with the news of his safe arrival, his parents gathered together the rest of their money and sent their 15-year-old son along the same route! After a month or more traveling and through a stack of paperwork and government agencies in Germany, the brothers were reunited in the home and allowed to live there together.

The supervisor of the home told me that once the brother arrived, the home took on an all new atmosphere. It had truly become a family, bonding not just the brothers, but all residents and supervisors.

That was just one heart-warming story of many from the group. All residents of that home wanted to learn German, learn a trade, and get integrated into society with a purpose. They all have hopes and dreams like any one of us, and they are willing to work hard to make those dreams come true.

I wanted to help them do just that, which is why Run4Refugees appealed to me so much. The goal of the project was that my partner and I would run 4,000 kilometers, the distance from Iran to Germany, with the project spanning from the January 1 until June 11.

Unfortunately, on New Year's Eve, the night before the project was to kick off, there was a lot of trouble in some cities in Germany, primarily Cologne, whereby women were molested by men on the streets; many (but not all) of those men were refugees. Needless to say, the attitude toward them was suddenly far from positive and welcoming. However, I still intended to give it my best effort and see what would happen. Not only would this project support the young men from the Sindbad home financially, our running team had essentially taken them under our wing and were looking for avenues to help them get integrated into their new culture via sport. Several of them were introduced into a boxing club since they had done some boxing where they grew up. One of them even took first place at a local competition at a folk festival. These guys were talented, and not just in boxing. Some of them were really good runners, finishing 10K races in about 38 minutes, which, for untrained 16-year-olds, is a fabulous time.

So, we started to bring a few of them along to our races, one of which is called the Spindellauf (spindle run). The location is in Regensburg's Donau Einkaufzentrum, one of the city's shopping malls, and gets its name from running up and down the five stories of the spiral ramp to the parking lots then through the upper and lower floors of the mall itself. The course is essentially a half marathon, 21 kilometers (13 miles), and is run in 14 laps. The race can be run alone or in a relay team of three runners.

I really love this event, as do most people in Regensburg, evident by the fact that registration maxes out in a day. It is also great for spectators because they get to see people running by 14 times! There are bands and a bar—it takes place at night. The start is at 8:30pm, after the mall closes, so there is a distinct party atmosphere.

I had run it on a relay team the past two years, ending up with finishes in the top three each year, but as often happens in the winter, one of my relay team members got sick the week before the race, and we needed a replacement. He was a really fast runner. I was hoping for another spot on the podium, but this news put that in question. So, my team leader and I talked about the alternatives and decided the best solution—for several reasons—would be to fill the slot with one of the refugees from Sindbad, a 16-year-old from Afghanistan, one of the guys in the group that I really clicked with. Plus, we thought his presence on the team with me would be a great idea in lieu of the Run4Refugees project, not to mention that he would totally have a great time!

But did we still have a chance for one of the top three slots? That had now become more or less irrelevant.

I offered to pick him up from the youth home and take him with me to the race. As I was driving there, I got a call from our team leader saying that one of our solo starters (planning to run the 21 km alone) was also sick and that I should ask at Sindbad for someone willing to take his place. When I arrived, I talked to one of the guys who I thought would be up for it and his reaction was, "Well, I've never run that far before, but I'll give it a try!"

Needless to say, driving in the car was a huge information exchange about how the race worked. My teammate had never run a relay, and the course was a little tricky. Once we got there, I ran him through the course and answered all his questions as best I could. His German was not yet great, and I was so happy that when he didn't comprehend something completely he asked me again and again until he was sure he understood.

Running at a full sprint through a shopping mall is an incredible feeling. The shop windows flying by on one side and fans lining the course and screaming for their teammates on the other. It really pumps you up, and the adrenaline is constantly at a peak. Temperatures inside the mall are about 20 degrees Celsius (70 °F) and outside about 5 degrees Celsius (40 °F), so the single starters were dressed with hats and long sleeves, and the sprinters in the relay teams in shorts and tanks! Climbing the parking ramp is tough, but it's over before you know it and then you are rewarded with its downhill pull and a minute to catch your breath before the final push to the baton transfer.

So, how did we do? After the very first lap, it was clear that the "A-Team" from our running team was really in another league (the guys were a professional triathlete and a 2:30 marathoner, respectively). But, surprise, surprise! Who was in second place? We were! And that is where we stayed for the entire race, slowly gaining ground over the 3rd place team with every lap. We were thrilled!

And our solo starter? Well, he not only finished his half marathon, but he also didn't stop when he should have and ended up running two extra laps! No one was quite sure if he didn't realize that he was done or just was having too much fun to stop.

Several days afterward, I talked to the leader of the Sindbad group home, and she said that the guys talked constantly about the race and were rarely seen without their finisher T-shirts.

So Run4Refugees was on, and although it was not as successful as I was hoping it would be, thanks to some skillful marketing ideas from Alex Müller at Bureau2+, several thousand Euros were raised through the project in total. The sum that I donated to Sindbad was matched by a local bike store, and six new mountain bikes were purchased by the home. Since they lived about 5 kilometers outside the city, this gave the boys more freedom to come and go as they needed and wanted. Watching them pick out the bikes and test ride them was one of the highlights of my year. None of them had ever owned a bike before. Yes, it was luxury, but after the horrors of what some of them had been through, it was a well-deserved gift. And I had the honor and pleasure of being Santa Claus for a day.

With the guys from Sindbad

Now back to the 100-kilometer race in Biel, Switzerland...

The 100-kilometer race of the Bieler Lauftage is one of the oldest and biggest of its kind, with a single 100-kilometer loop. That year, there were a whopping 830 finishers of the 100-kilometer race alone. There is also a 56-kilometer (35 miles) ultramarathon, a half marathon, and a night marathon, bringing more than 4,500 runners to Biel on a Friday night in June. The atmosphere at the start is absolutely electric. There are just so many people around that the city is in complete party mode. The course is relatively flat, with only four significant rises, and in total there are less than 1,000 meters of positive elevation. Flatter races over that distance would be hard to find.

Lucky number 100 for the 100-kilometer race

I drove down to Biel, Switzerland, with my husband and two youngest children on a Thursday, stopping quickly in the city to pick up my start number (lucky number 100!), before driving to an inn about 20 minutes outside the city. I chose the inn because it had a swimming pool and tennis courts, which the kids could use to keep entertained all day Friday while I could just rest, since the start of the race was 10pm on Friday night. We sat at the pool on race day and worked out my strategy for food, drink, and supplies. My husband was to meet me at predetermined sites *en route* in our VW van, with the backseat folded down as a make-shift bed for the kids who had their sleeping bags and pillows set up for an exciting night of following mama 100 kilometers through the Swiss countryside!

By 7pm the van was packed, and we were ready to go. As I said, the race begins at 10pm, which obviously magnifies the party aspect because, well, those who are not running are partying on a Friday night. Even as you run through the smaller villages along the course at midnight, 1, 2, and even 3am, there are people out there cheering the runners on (naturally encouraged a bit by the

My cheering squad from Sindbad

local wine). On the drive into the city I got a message from the woman in charge of Sindbad. She sent me a photo of three of the youths holding signs, reading, "Go, Holly, Go!" What a feeling of satisfaction and joy.

Upon arriving in the city, we met up with my Run4Refugees project partner, Tom, and took some photos together before finding a place to sit down. We planned to run the first 30 kilometers together before he would take off and run his much faster tempo.

My "crew" and me

The sky was beautiful, and the crowd was charged, but the tension could almost be cut with a knife. Most runners had backpacks with drinks, gels, and extra gear, but I knew that the refreshment stations had almost everything I needed, and what they didn't have I'd get from Frank in the van. There were 18 refreshment stations on the course spaced about 5 kilometers apart. They offered a choice of beverages from water and Gatorade to tea, hot broth, and Pepsi, and a smorgasbord of food, including three different kinds of sports bars and gels, as well as bananas, apples, oranges, bread, and pretzels. What more could you ask for? There was even a coffee bar set up near kilometer 50.

And if that wasn't enough, runners were allowed to have a bike supporter, which could certainly be helpful in carrying extra clothes or shoes if the temperatures change drastically or in case of heavy rain, but in terms of food supply, the race organizers had it covered.

The first several kilometers weaved through the city where there were people everywhere cheering us on. It was tempting to run a fast tempo, but we had to keep track of pace and forcibly slow down so that we didn't overdo it right from the start.

Once out of the city, we ran through some fields and small villages, and since it was relatively early, there were still quite a few fans, not only in the villages, as there was even a party tent set up in a field. As we ran by them, they were much more consumed by the party than the runners or the race, and they also didn't seem to be bothered by the lightening moving our way nor the ferocious wind that was beginning to pick up.

As luck would have it, the direction we were running headed right into the storm. The weather forecast had been for clear skies for most of the night with a high probability for showers around 4 or 5am. This would have been ok, but to get walloped by a torrential downpour with howling wind after only an hour was not what any of us expected or were prepared for. I was cold and wet and miserable. The rain was bad enough, but the wind was just depressing at kilometer 15 of a 100-kilometer race. We then entered the city of Aarberg, home of the famous covered wooden bridge, and the mood lightened. The wooden bridge was built in 1568 to span the Aare River, and at the time it was the only river crossing between Bern and Büren. The bridge is breathtaking; the design exquisitely unique; and because it lies at kilometer 17 on the race course, almost all runners cross it before midnight, still quite early, so the bridge is packed with fans. The reverberating echoes of cheers were incredible. And since the bridge is covered, it protected us from the rain! If only for a few moments.

Soon after I was relieved to see the white VW van was in sight; I ran over and immediately stripped out of my soaking wet shirt. I put on a dry shirt and my rain jacket. It was so nice to be warm again!

It was already dark, but I didn't get my headlamp from the van, which I regretted soon afterward. Running in the dark on foreign ground is difficult. If we were running simply on the streets it would be ok, but there were paths dotted with holes and puddles, and I kept having to stay with other people who already had their headlamps on. An hour later, when I saw Frank and the kids again, my headlamp was the first thing I collected.

My partner, Tom, kept edging ahead, or I kept falling behind, I couldn't be sure which. Then he'd circle around and come back to me again. I told him to please go and run his own tempo. It didn't make sense to stay with me. But he is one to stick with "the plan," and he kept by my side until the 30-kilometer mark before shooting off into the darkness ahead of me.

My supply vehicle, a.k.a. kids camp

Although having someone to talk to helps pass the time immeasurably, I was relieved not to have the added burden of holding him back, and I felt more comfortable finally being able to run my own tempo. Usually some type of mantra takes hold of my mind during a race, a song that I like or a motivational thought, but during this race a song that I DO NOT like kept running through my head, the one with the lyrics, "My name's Blurryface and I care what you think." Ugh. Hours upon end this ran through my head. But my daughter loves the song, so that gave me strength and perseverance. There's a reason for everything.

I was wearing a running hat that had a visor with my headlamp on top of it, so the light pattern it made on the ground before me was bizarre, creating a kind of tunnel vision. That, in combination with the dark visor just above my eyes, made me feel like I was looking through the windscreen of a motorcycle helmet. I tried to shut out all thoughts and go into a trance. That worked for short periods of time.

I had to set short-term goals. What will I eat at the next stop? Drink? Occasionally the need to pee kept me entertained. Where can I go? For several kilometers I would search for the best place to quickly duck off to the side and hide behind some bushes. It had to be the perfect spot, well protected but not more than a few meters out of my way. This helped me pass the time.

When I was at kilometer 60, along the section of the Emmendamm, nicknamed the Ho Chi Min trail, a single-track trail with uneven ground and heavily grown in with trees and bushes, the second downpour hit. And it was very dark in there. Dark, heavy rain, uneven terrain, puddles. It was tricky, but I think that was my favorite part of the whole course. At one point while running through there I could hear singing in the distance ahead of me, but there were no lights, no villages, and not even any roads going through that section. As I got closer, I saw three men (quite drunk) who had driven through the fields and had climbed up to the edge of the path, in the pouring rain, and they were singing and cheering us on like crazed hooligans. The runners were so uplifted that we were singing and cheering right back!

As I exited the Emmendamm the sun began to rise, and the next time I saw Frank and the kids I stopped to change my shoes and socks. I was soaked through to my skin. Time for the Hokas! I also put on another shirt and jacket. Only 30 kilometers to go!

Time to get out of those wet shoes

Shortly after that, as I was running along a semi-major road, I saw the van in the distance parked at a café. I was surprised because I hadn't expected to see my family again so soon, and then as I got nearer I saw my husband running out with an espresso in his hand for me! What luxury service! The women sitting at a table outside were smiling from ear to ear.

The kids were awake now, and each time they would park at a meeting point, they would run or bike in my direction. Amelia had her bike which Frank took out for both the kids to use each time we stopped. So, when I saw them in the distance I knew it wasn't long before my next energy break.

Kid's entourage

Amelia accompanying me on her BMX

By now I'd begun to sit down for a minute or two each time I met up with the van, just long enough to let my legs rest for a moment, but not long enough to let them stiffen up. As I sat, Amelia would serve me. Gels were working really well for me during this race. That is not always the case, and sometimes during a marathon I have to force them down toward the end. I also had my cashews roasted in soy sauce, Millenium bars, and of course my oatmeal milk, the best energy supply that I know of for ultrarunning—a drink and energy source in one! I also took a few salt tablets periodically after kilometer 60, just to be sure.

At kilometer 75, Amelia met me on her bike. She'd ridden about two kilometers uphill to where I was, and that meant we had a nice two kilometers downhill together. Frank and the kids were such a huge support. The kids were in great spirits, and Frank, too, even though he hadn't slept at all that night either.

The next time I saw them was when Robert came running toward me at about kilometer 85; I was happy to see him and relieved to know that I'd soon get to another rest stop, but then after each turn when I still didn't see the van I wondered where it was. "Robert, how far did you run?" "A really long way, mama," he replied. It turns out he'd run about 2 kilometers to reach me. This was unfortunately a tough spot for me because when I saw him my mind and body registered a rest; I had assumed not more than a couple hundred meters, but it took an eternity to finally get to the van. As I sat down in the back, I was not doing well. This was kilometer 87, and the lowest point for me in the race. I lay back to elevate my legs briefly; they hurt. I wasn't sure what to eat or drink either. It was not a question of whether to continue—I knew I would finish somehow—but I needed to focus. After probably about three minutes, the longest stop I'd had by far, Frank forced me on the road again, knowing that it was the best thing to just keep in motion.

The last time I saw the van before the finish was 5 kilometers later at kilometer 92, and I was doing much better. One foot in front of the other. Amelia met me 500 meters before the van and ran alongside me. Frank took a few photos of us as we ran side by side. Another gel, some oatmeal milk, and some water, and I was on my way again—right into the third rain storm. Another downpour. I was completely soaked. But I knew I was close, and I was so looking forward to that finish line. But why wasn't I in the city yet? I kept expecting to be running the last several kilometers through city streets, but I was still on trails until about kilometer 97.

Running with my Amelia at kilometer 92

When I finally hit city street pavement, I began to feel lighter and run with ease. Only a few more curves before I could hear the music at the finish line. My kids came out and joined me for the last hundred meters. "Robert, don't run in front of me or I'll trip over you!" I had to warn him because I wasn't all that much in control of my movements anymore. So, with a child on either side, I crossed the finish line. 100 kilometers in 12 hours and 17 minutes. Far from my 11-hour goal, but an amazing accomplishment for a very happy mama.

I sat down with the kids behind the finish line while Frank went to get the van, and when he came back, I could barely stand and walk the 50 meters to it. I needed help getting in. My muscles had cramped up. I told Frank I needed to collect a finisher's shirt, and he went off to look for them. He came back with a size small that looked very small, so we drove together to the hall where they were giving them out and Frank practically carried me inside to try on the medium, which fit better. And I was really happy I got one. The finisher T-shirts were available in both a men's and women's cut, and they had cool colors, large print, and black stripes on the sides which, as all ladies know, is "slimming;" we like that. Such great finisher shirts are, unfortunately, not the case everywhere, and most disappointingly was the one that I got from the Marathon des Sables this year—plain white, with tiny print on the front reading "Finisher" and even tinier print under that reading "Marathon des Sables!" And nothing on the back! I mean, if someone runs 257 kilometers through the Sahara Desert, they have earned the right to slap it all over town! So anyway, the medal at Biel was really nice, too. It is heavy and of good quality with lots of fine detail, but what I really like about it is the neck band. It is not a simple red- or blue-and-white-striped band, but rather it is bright and colorful and has that beautiful Swiss flag proudly displayed.

Biel was a great race. Well organized and relatively easy to run. I would have enjoyed it much more had it been run in daylight so that I could take in the gorgeous panorama of the countryside and lattice timber-framed farm houses.

Oh well, you can't have everything, I suppose. But the memories that my family and I did take away from Biel will stay with us for a lifetime.

100km Biel finisher shirt and medal

CHAPTER 22

BOSTON MARATHON 2013: THE RACE

Most long-distance races have some aspect of the unknown which inspires and brings people back to run in them despite the physical difficulties. How will my body react to the distance in the heat or cold? Has my training been adequate to keep my planned pace? Do I have enough calories to get me through? And what if it rains? But no one goes to a race and wonders if there is going to be a terrorist attack at the finish line.

The Boston Marathon is an icon, a pillar in the sport of long-distance running. It is the world's oldest annual marathon, having been run since 1897, inspired by the first Olympic Marathon in 1896. It is held every year on Patriot's Day, the third Monday in April. I can still remember sitting in front of the television as a kid, watching Billy Rodgers streak through Boston in his split nylon shorts, the crowds going wild at the finish.

In the few days prior to flying to Boston, I still couldn't quite believe what I was about to do: Going to run in the world's oldest annual marathon, the Boston Marathon, the most incredible marathon in the world.

And then the day came to say goodbye to my family for a week and, sitting on the flight from Munich to Boston, all I kept thinking was that I was flying in the wrong direction. Away from my kids. Away from my home. To run 26.2 miles on another continent. Why was I doing that to myself? To my family?

Things got better once I arrived. The city lights of Boston, the Sox game on the radio, seeing my dad, a good night's sleep, friends, shopping. Two days before the race I visited Sheryl, one of my "oldest" friends, and just before I left her, she placed a small, silver object in my hand—a guardian angel—and she told me to carry it with me during the race.

My first thought was, "Oh, my gosh, this thing is heavy." I mean, I buy racing shoes that are just grams lighter than my trainers to save weight over the long haul. Now I need to carry this? But, be it sentimentality or superstition, I found a way to pin it into my power gel belt since I didn't have any pockets in my shorts or in the belt.

So the angel came with me to Boston. Little did I know then that I would really need her.

The next day was the marathon expo at the Hynes Convention

My guardian angel

ULTRAMARATHON MOM

Center on Bolyston Street, just steps away from the starting line! It was crazy, as expected. I was thrilled just to be there, pick up my race number, check out the other runners, and get into the race excitement. My dad and aunt Cathy insisted that I had to have the official marathon jacket, and they bought one for me. Then we got to see Billy Rodgers—Boston Billy!

I even had the opportunity to meet one of my greatest inspirations in endurance running—Dean Karnazes. I talked to him for a couple of minutes, and he signed my copy of his book, *Ultramarathon Man*.

Katherine Switzer was also there. She was the first woman to run Boston with a race number in 1967. But, registered as "K.V. Switzer," the organizers didn't realize she was a woman until during the race, at which point they tried to rip off her race number while she was running and have her ejected. They were unsuccessful, and she finished the race, which essentially started the revolution of women in marathons. (Thanks, K.V.)

After leaving the expo, we walked over to take a look at the finish line, which was absolutely inundated with media, tourists, and runners. Again, the goosebumps—for about the tenth time that day!

After a great pasta dinner with my family, I was in bed by 10:00. And up at 4:00. Ok, so I was still jet-lagged...and very excited.

My aunt dropped me off at Boston Commons at 7:00am where I was immediately enveloped in an endless serpentine mass of runners trying to load onto yellow school buses. An hour later I was sitting on a bus with three other women: Katy from Utah,

Berenice from Ohio (originally from Mexico City), and Sharon from western Massachusetts. I still keep in touch with all of them.

The bus ride took an hour; I laughed my ass off the whole way. I almost forgot what it felt like to laugh so much (the German sense of humor is a bit different than that of my own culture; they don't use sarcasm so much), and my face muscles hurt by the time I got to Hopkinton.

Once arriving at the Athlete's Village at Hopkinton High School, the four of us headed straight for the lines at the porta-potties. And that was where Katy pointed out a bizarre sight to me: fully-armed security guards on the roof of the school. What the hell?

We lost Sharon at the toilets, and after packing down a bagel, a banana, and whatever else she could get her hands on, Berenice left for the starting blocks. Katy and I hung out a bit. She was still telling jokes. She'd taken a photo of a male runner with a banana sticking out of his pocket: "Is that a banana in your pocket or are you just happy to see me run?" We were checking out the other runners. I've never seen such an amazing collection of athletes at any of the races I'd been to. Everyone looked like a professional. Unbelievably fit from head to toe. Then it was time for Katy and me to head out, too, so we walked the 0.7 miles to the starting line together.

I was in the second of three waves in the marathon. The first started at 10:00, mine started twenty minutes later, and the third at 10:40. There were nine starting blocks in each wave with 1,000 runners per block, and I was in the ninth block, so I was pretty far from the starting line when the horn sounded. This year, for the first time in 117 years, the marathon was started by an air horn instead of a gun in memory of the school children killed in Newtown, Connecticut. We stood with anticipation for a couple of minutes after the start, then we slowly started edging forward, sometimes at a slow jog, stopping short again, back to a walk, and finally a few yards before the starting line we all started into a steady run. Total exhilaration. Of course, there were quite a few spectators, but I didn't risk looking around much for fear of tripping over one of my fellow runners. We were so packed into the narrow road that you had no choice but to run with the pace of the pack. Slowing down or passing people was not an option. There was no space. Countless times other runners stepped on my heels, and I on theirs. I kept waiting for someone to trip. But thankfully no one did.

At about 5 kilometers (3 miles), things started to open up. At that point, after going up and down several (not minor) hills, I already knew that it was not going to be a PR (personal record) day. My goal pace was 5:15 minutes per kilometer (8:30 per mile), but since we were always either ascending or descending a (not minor) hill, my pace was usually at about 5:00 or 5:40, respectively. So eventually I stopped looking at my watch and just looked around me.

The spectators were great. We crossed through several small towns where families were gathered on their front lawns for barbecues (though the smell of cooked meat while running, or doing anything for that matter, does not appeal to me), but it was fun to watch, and they were all busy handing out cut oranges, water, beer, bananas, and sticks of Vaseline (if you run, you can relate).

A lot of the runners wore shirts with inscriptions dedicating their run to loved ones. One runner was videotaping himself as he ran, shirtless, with full commentary. I passed him a couple of times since he kept stopping to videotape himself.

Dorothy from Oz, in a checkered blue dress and red sneakers, ran by with a sign on her back that read, "There's no place like Boston."

As I mentioned, everyone held the same pace for the first 5 kilometers (3 miles), and once it opened up, quite a few runners began to pass me. This went on, and on, and on for miles. I was really wondering if I had undertrained? Why were so many people passing me? But, then, at about the 20-kilometer (12 miles) mark, everyone settled down, very few passed me, and we were mostly all running the same pace for the next 10 kilometers. We ran through Wellesley College, where you face the "Scream Tunnel" or the "Wall of Sound," in other words, hundreds of college women screaming so loudly that you could hear them a half mile away. Many of them held signs offering kisses: "Kiss a Chemist;" "Kiss me I'm from Texas;" "Kiss me I'm horny." Seriously. A kiss for male or female runners. It didn't matter. Two girls were holding signs in front of them, but with bare legs and arms, so that they looked as though they had nothing on. I have no idea what the signs said, as I'm sure the other runners also didn't, since we were too busy trying to run past the girls to see if there was anything behind them. There was. They had short-shorts and tank tops on. Cute idea.

At kilometer 29 I passed Team Hoyt, the father and son racing team (i.e., father pushing son in a wheelchair). They had run 30 Boston Marathons and multiple Ironman distance triathlons. A bronze statue was dedicated in their honor on April 8, 2013, near the start of the Boston Marathon in Hopkinton, Massachusetts.

When I passed them, they were walking, but were being showered with attention from both runners and spectators.

Shortly thereafter I heard a very familiar voice call out my name. Dad. Anyone who knows my father knows that his voice is unmistakable. My legs instinctively changed course, and I ran over to him for a big hug, barely missing a beat, then back to work.

Finally the magic mark came at about kilometer 30 (mile 20); it was my turn to shine. I started passing people. I wasn't speeding up. Actually, I was probably slowing down, but just not quite as much as the others. Relief. My training was good after all. Perfect timing because the hills of Newton were up next. Four of them, one right after another, culminating with the infamous Heartbreak Hill. As I've said, the entire course was hilly, right from the start. By the time I'd gotten to Heartbreak Hill at kilometer 31, it was more like a molehill than a mountain. And that was where I really passed a lot of people. Then as I crested the peak of Heartbreak, that's where I saw the best spectator-held sign of the day—a young woman was holding a large handmade sign which read, "You think your legs are hurting...my arms are killing me!" I smiled, we caught each other's eyes, and I gave her a slight nod (all I could muster). She smiled back.

Boston College was next. And the fans there didn't disappoint. They were loud, they were crazy, they were hilarious, and for a few minutes they took my mind off the aches and pains that were slowing creeping into my body.

We then ran down into the city and through Kenmore Square which was loaded with Red Sox fans who had spilled out from Fenway after the game against Tampa Bay. By that point in the race, the final mile, I was so exhausted that I barely noticed; it had all come down to concentrating on the basics—one foot in front of the other. I kept looking for the turn, the cutover to Boylston and the last several hundred meters, and when I finally made it around the corner, I could see the finish line. I positioned myself right in the middle of the road and gave it all I had. There were thousands of spectators, flags were flying, the sun was shining, cameras were everywhere, and as I crossed that fabulously painted line at Copley Square there were tears in my eyes and a smile on my face.

I could hardly believe it.

I had just run the Boston Marathon.

CHAPTER 23

BOSTON MARATHON 2013: THE BOMBING

When I crossed the finish line in Boston, I was on cloud nine, but the primary emotion was that of relief because I could finally stop running. I was completely, physically empty. Like every other runner who'd just finished, I walked wearily forward and filtered into the mass of exhausted human beings as we wove our way farther up Boylston Street to be greeted and cared for by the B.A.A. volunteers. We first collected water and HeatSheet blankets. I was freezing by the time I'd gotten mine; it's amazing how fast your body cools down. They were also handing out stickers to bind the front of the HeatSheets closed, but I didn't have the energy or coordination to take it in my hand and stick it on, so I just stood there like a child and had one of the volunteers attach it for me. I wasn't the only runner to do this, and a smile was all I could summon as thanks. Then we got our medals, a bottle of Gatorade, and a bag of food. The volunteers handing out these items were so friendly and were joking with us; they were clearly having a blast themselves. But several times I had to stop and bend over, holding onto my knees to rest. I knew I needed some energy in the form of food, but I was too spent to do anything more than stay in motion. The buses that held our bags full of clothing and personal items were still ahead, so I pulled my HeatSheet blanket as tight as I could around me and searched for yellow school bus #23. A few minutes later I'd found it and received my bag, then slipped behind the bus to put on some warm clothes. I peeled off my sweaty shirt and replaced it with a warm, dry, long-sleeved one, and a jacket. Another female runner who'd come back there with me saw me take off my shirt (of course I had a sports bra underneath) and said that she was too embarrassed to do that since there were so many people around. I told her it's like giving birth…you're so desperate you don't give a damn how many people are in the room. She laughed and made a quick change.

From there I returned to the middle of Boylston because I needed to go back in the direction of the finish line to get to the runners' exits. I was feeling better since I was now warm, and I was enjoying watching the other runners, all of us sensing our mutual satisfaction and camaraderie. The atmosphere was charged with excitement, yet very controlled and peaceful. I didn't want it to end.

And then in a moment it all suddenly changed.

There was a deafening noise. I looked up and saw a ball of white smoke rising into the air on the right side of the road on the far side of the finish line. Everyone around me stood still. My first thought was that it was part of the event, a celebratory canon shot or something. It didn't really seem to make sense. It didn't fit in with the scene, in the atmosphere. I stood for a moment to see what would happen next. But nothing did, so then all the runners and I slowly began moving again; I was only able to take another step or two before there was a second loud noise and the accompanying smoke. But this time... I knew. And so did everyone around me. The woman next to me said, "Oh, no. This is not good." We began to move faster in all directions. I took the next street off of Boylston in the direction where I was supposed to exit and meet my family. It was only a matter of a minute or two before the sirens began; ambulances were being brought into the area, one right after the other. There were still thousands of runners trying to get to the exits, and the police were urging us to the sides of the roads so that the ambulances could get through. And they were coming at unbelievable speeds. I was trying to push back against the crowds so as not to get hit by one of the rescue vehicles flying through. Panic began to spread rapidly. I was exhausted and began to get scared. Tears welled in my eyes, and I was shaking. When I finally got to the runner's exit, there were men there who were telling us to get back. To go the other way. But I knew that I was supposed to meet my aunt and father just around the corner. I didn't want to go the other way.

I wasn't sure what to do, but then decided to take the risk and moved forward, despite the warnings; I squeezed myself through the metal barriers. When I was outside of the runner's-only area, I began to see spectators and families. There were parents running down the street with small kids tucked under their arms. I felt a brief wave of relief that my kids, for once, weren't there. I also noticed many people who had no idea that there was something wrong. More than a block behind Boylston, they had probably not seen or heard anything. When some of them looked at me and saw the fear in my face along with the screaming ambulances, they knew something wasn't right. I tried to cover my face; I didn't want to scare anyone since I wasn't at all sure what was going on. Maybe (hopefully) it was nothing? But I was just so exhausted after the race that I couldn't help but let my emotions out. I finally made it to the place where I'd planned to meet my dad and aunt—under the large letter M. But they weren't there. Now I was really scared. What if something happened to them? And where do I go now?

I took out my phone and tried to call my aunt Cathy, but the call didn't go through. I checked my messages, and she had sent me a text, but it didn't make any sense to me. Later that night I recalled the text on my phone; it read: "I'm at the m sign on corner." How could I not have understood that? But my mind couldn't process anything; my cell phone felt burdensomely heavy and looked to me like a strange device that I couldn't even begin to understand. Then, finally, after what seemed like an eternity but was probably only a minute or two, I heard someone calling my name. It was Cathy. She had briefly gone to look for me. I was *so* relieved. I pretty much fell into her arms. My dad was right behind her. I said, "We have to get out of here," and we started walking in the direction of Copley Plaza. Cathy practically had to carry me the first couple of blocks; I was so completely drained. My poor father was struggling behind us. I knew I needed to call home and let them know I was safe. So at the next corner we stopped for a second, and I called Frank. Thankfully the call went through, and it was a panacea to hear his calm voice answer on the other end of the line. I said in a panic, "I'm ok! I'm ok!" but at that point he hadn't heard any of the news yet, and he didn't know what I was talking about, but then he heard the sirens and mayhem in the background of my call, and he knew that something was wrong. I told him what I knew and promised I'd call him again shortly since we had to keep moving; we just wanted to get away. Cathy's car was parked in the garage under the Copley Plaza Mall on Boylston. We couldn't get to it from Bolyston because the roads were now closed off, so we thought maybe we could get there via the glass overpass one block away. The ambulances were starting to line up, and the police vehicles kept coming in, every make of vehicle from Hummers to full-size pick-ups, suited up with flashing lights behind the grill.

Once we finally made it into the Copley Plaza Mall, I began to feel better. Safer. It was quiet. We found a bench, and I finally got to sit down for the first time since finishing the race, almost an hour earlier. But sadly there were other runners in there who hadn't been able to finish. The mall was on Boylston about a quarter mile from the finish line, and some of them were stopped right outside and went in there for safety. They didn't have any warm clothes, or water, or food. I gave my foil HeatSheet to a woman in a tank top and shorts who told me she was stopped a half mile from the finish. Others were given tablecloths from one of the restaurants and had themselves wrapped up in those. People were walking around with blank stares, texting their friends and loved ones since the cell phone network had since been shut down (apparently for fear of a triggered explosion).

We then learned that we were under lockdown. No one else allowed in the building and no one out. We had to "ask" to go to the bathroom. There was a bank or an electronics shop (can't remember which) in the mall, which was closed, but had a television that we could see through the glass storefront with *CNN* reporting live about the events in Boston. We were getting our information from that and from our friends who were texting us about what was going on from Internet or other news sources.

Then we got the news in a text from Frank: Two dead. Forty injured.

That was the first mention I'd heard about casualties. Oh, Lord.

My aunt Cathy looked at me seriously and said, "You know, we are sitting here under the tallest building in Boston." A perfect target.

"Maybe we should get out of here," I replied. And that was timely, too. Since, just then, after about an hour and a half of lockdown, we were told that they were evacuating the building. We had to leave. But where to? There were no trains or buses. We didn't want Lou, Cathy's husband to come get us, because, really, we weren't sure how safe it was downtown. So we just headed out and away. We kept walking and decided to try to flag down a taxi or maybe hitch a ride. But of course, every taxi that went by was already occupied. Plus, most of the streets where we were had already been closed to public traffic and were cordoned off by police with flashing lights. The undercover police cars were still coming in at a constant rate, and this was about three hours after the explosions. Where were they all coming from?

My poor father, at 70 years old and with weak lungs, kept having to take short breaks. But it's amazing what the human body can endure under such circumstances. After walking for a while, we came across a bench, and my father sat down. It was then that Cathy spied a taxi at the next intersection that was empty. She hailed him and had to do some wrangling to get him to take us to Winchester—normally a 10-minute drive, but under those circumstances it would be about an hour. We climbed into the cab and breathed a sigh of relief. There were road closures and detours, but we didn't care; we knew it was over for us. We listened to the radio in the taxi, and there was news of an incident at the JFK Library in Dorchester. Another explosion? They weren't sure.

I then realized that the small toe on my left foot hurt, so I took off my shoe to find a fat blood blister. Hard to believe how I did not feel that until four hours after finishing a race. Just goes to show how powerful the mind is.

All in all, I was one of the lucky ones that day to have come home safe and without injury (except for a meager blood blister), and I'm grateful that my father and aunt who were there to watch me finish were also not hurt, though my dad had been in the vicinity of the explosions but on the opposite side of the street just minutes before. My heart breaks for those who were injured or killed and for their families and loved ones. And quite naturally I carry some guilty feelings—running is a very selfish sport, and most of those injured were there to watch us, to cheer us on. My sympathies are also with the B.A.A. and the volunteers who organized and implemented such an enormous event that flowed with perfection and was simply meant for the enjoyment of not only the runners, but also the spectators, volunteers, and the entire city of Boston. After seeing the quick reaction of the medical workers, hearing about runners donating blood, and all the outpouring of support for those injured, I know that for every ignorant, self-serving, hate-filled human being, there are thousands upon thousands of good, loving, helpful, and wonderful souls.

I know that I will always carry memories of that day with me— good and bad. Although before the race I said it would be my one-and-only Boston, I've since changed my mind. I know that I'll be back to run the Boston Marathon again, an opinion probably shared by most of the runners on April 15, 2013.

Yes, Boston is strong.

CHAPTER 24

A 24-HOUR BIKE RACE

As I've mentioned before, biking is an essential way for runners to build up endurance while sparing the body the jarring forces created by hitting the pavement with every step. I'm not an experienced biker, but I have always used mountain biking as cross-training, endurance training, or just to have fun with friends.

Since I'm always open for an adventure, when I was asked a few years ago to participate in a 24-hour bike race, I immediately said "Yes!" Then my inner voice of reason said, "What the hell do you know about bike racing? What do you even know about bikes for that matter?" That stubborn inner voice had a point, so I signed myself up for a bike mechanics seminar and was on my way!

Then I found out that I'd also need a new bike. Oh. That was unexpected. Just the year before I had bought a triathlon bike (strictly aerobars), which would not be allowed in this race. I had a lot of friends, including my own husband, who participated in triathlons, so at the time I thought that triathlons might be something for me, too. After acquiring a secondhand Cervelo and a season of training, I had set my sights on my first triathlon challenge, the Volksdistanz of the 3MUC Triathlon Munich: 400 meters swimming, 20 kilometers biking, and a 5-kilometer run. Why this one? Because it had the shortest swimming distance I could find, and I'd only learned to swim the crawl 12 months before. Also, it was to be held in the Regatta Course in Munich which was built for the 1972 Olympics! How idyllic! Crystal clear water, easy to sight—in other words, a very controlled situation, or so I thought.

The water temperature was 17.4 degrees Celsius (63 °F) at the start. Very cold. Almost everyone had full wetsuits on. I had a neoprene swimsuit, so arms and from the hips down, I was fully exposed. I knew this was a bad sign. I jumped in and my body experienced a brief shock. *Holy shit!*

Moments later we were off. The first ten meters were great! Calm, easy, super. But after I got a mouthful of water, panic set in, and it was over for me with the crawl. I tried the breaststroke (which I can't really do), so I tried the backstroke (ditto), and then I tried the simply-move-forward-without-drowning stroke and found that to work the best. After about 100 meters I started looking for the rescue boat…no need to look for long because they already had me in their sights and were moving closer to my position, clearly thinking I was a possible candidate for a ride home. I don't honestly know how I finished the swim. I was one of the last ones out of the water. Somehow I got through in a whopping 12:59.

Then onto the bike! There were people on mountain bikes, so I knew I had an advantage with the holy Cervelo. The course was four laps around the regatta with 2.5-kiolometer passages on each side and 150 meters at each end. The out loop was into the wind where I simply tried to stay over 30 km/h and the back loop had the wind in our favor where I tried to keep it over 35 km/h. I was constantly passing people. I began to get some confidence back and really enjoyed it. Total time with the two transitions: 39:51. Goal was under 40…I was in the game!

Finally I was in my running sneaks, and after a few wobbly moments, I got into my rhythm on the run. It was a two-lap course, and a little tricky—some trails, some grassy spots, some pavement, lots of turns. But, since I train for endurance, even after the catastrophic swim and the bike, I was still feeling strong, especially on the second lap where I passed lots of runners. Before I knew it, after five kilometers and 21:54 on my feet, the fun was over. Cumulative time was 1:14:44. My goal was under 1:20. Satisfied. Relieved. And I was on the podium as third in my age group! Hallelujah, miracles do happen!

But after that disaster of a swim, that was enough of triathlons for me, and I haven't done one since, which is also why the holy Cervelo was sold, and it didn't take long to find another secondhand bike, albeit a racing machine, for the 24-hour race.

Now that I had my bike, my training had begun. This primarily entailed getting used to the bike and working on endurance. The bike itself rode like a dream, and I soon gained confidence riding at high speeds and longer and longer distances. For endurance I began training twice a day…usually a run and a ride, two rides, or yoga and swimming thrown in the mix. I kept my fingers crossed that I could avoid injury. And, a week before the race, I ended my training with a hard, four-hour session before five days of easy regeneration.

The 24-hour race takes part in and around the medieval city of Kelheim. There are 300 teams of five who camp in specifically allotted locations in the city for the weekend. The 16.4-kilometer course starts and ends in the center and as in any relay, one biker on the team rides at a time, then passes off the transponder to the next teammate who is waiting in the transition zone....then, repeat, uhhh....for 24 hours. Thus, the team that wins is the one with the most full laps within the 24-hour period.

Our two teams before the start of the 24-hour bike race
© Armin Wolf Laufteam

There was a mass start at 2pm, but I had some time to wait since I was the fourth biker on our team. I was so nervous while waiting at the exchange, but then I saw my teammate and went into action. I grabbed the water bottle which held the transponder, slipped it into my bottle rack, clipped into my pedals, and was off. My start was good...through the beer tent. (Did I mention the transfer zone was in a massive beer tent full of hundreds of cheering, beer-drinking enthusiasts, who were screaming encouragement as we rode way too fast through a narrow course over slippery cobblestone? Well, it was.) The adrenaline raced through my blood right from the start. Armin Wolf was again the moderator, and I heard him announce my name as I clipped into my pedals, "The American...Holly Zimmermann...Extreme Athlete (really?...that sounds cool)...Finisher of the Zugspitz Extremberglauf and the Boston Marathon..." And then I was out of earshot and pummeling on toward the "climb." The first six kilometers are uphill—think steep, serpentine.

Fans in the medieval city of Kelheim sitting outside of the beer tent

I passed several people on the incline, and I noticed a small contingent of my conquests organizing themselves behind me. I could see that there was a biker behind me only centimeters from my back wheel. OMG. I just kept my head down, stayed in the saddle, and tried to keep pushing but not overdoing the pace. Then before I knew it, the summit was in sight...visible by a

At the bike lockers after an adrenaline-pumping lap
© Armin Wolf Laufteam

huge inflated-balloon-type red gate over the road. A party tent was pitched at the steepest part with music and super fabulous fans that were there all through the night! The group was still assembled directly behind me, so I eased off to the inside and motioned that it was time for one of them to take the lead. I almost wished I hadn't; we were heading downhill at speeds approaching 60 km/h (37 mph)! I was with this group for a while, but at the sharp 90-degree turn at the bottom of the hill, I was overly conservative and hit the brakes too much...didn't want to crash into those hay bales...and quick as a flash, my group was gone, and I couldn't catch them. I fought most of the last seven kilometers of the course on my own, and when I came into the finish and passed off the bottle to the next biker, I was in a bit of a shock. Holy moly! I needed to process what I'd just experienced. In training I'd never reached those speeds, and I'd never drafted like that. I asked several of my teammates for advice. "Where should I focus my sight when I am riding in a group?...at the rear wheel of the biker just centimeters in front of me?...at the rider two ahead?...or further up the road?" Everywhere, I was told. Great, that's freaking (oops) helpful.

My second lap was tough as I never really found a group that I could stay with, and I spent a lot of energy trying to keep up speed. But the third lap was fabulous. I had a group the whole way, and we rotated like pros (or so we envisioned). As we came into the finish, we all congratulated each other before heading back to our respective "camps."

Then came my first lap in the dark. There was a full moon that night, but as it was overcast, we didn't benefit from it. I had a great headlamp and front and rear lights on the bike (which were required), but it was still dark. Once out of the downtown, there was no street lighting. Things were confusing. Every biker had different lighting—some with headlamps, others not. Some with bizarrely patterned LED bulbs on their arms, vests, helmets, and whatever. I was never really sure what I was seeing. And did I mention speeds at 60 to even 70 km/h? But not at night, right? Think again. Yes, at night, too. This race was *insane!* But I loved it!

I had about two hours of recovery between rides. After every lap, I had pretty much the same routine: drink water, change into dry clothes, drink water, eat, drink water, and then rest while drinking water. One and a half to two liters of water after every lap! The two-hour rest period was not easy because you were so full of adrenaline when you finished that you just wanted to keep going, but you slowly started to relax, and then you got tired, and then you started to contemplate things. Not good. I was afraid to lie down because I thought that if I slept then I would not be really alert when I woke up. But if I didn't sleep? That could be worse. So, at 3am, I finally lay down for an hour. It was very quiet in the tent, but there was still so much going on that I could only rest but not sleep, which I was satisfied with. At around 4am, as I was stumbling around in the dark trying to get my gear on for my next lap, I slipped into my bike shoes and right into something wet and squishy...a big, fat slug! Or what used to be one. I scooped its remains out with my finger, wiped off my sock, and tried to ignore the disgustingness of it all before heading out for my last ride in the dark, for which I was rewarded in the end with a breathtaking sunrise as I came over the bridge into the old city. Yes, Grateful Dead, you said it, at least I was enjoying the ride.

Still smiling after nearly a day at the race
© Armin Wolf Laufteam

My seventh lap started out the same as always: passing several riders except for the elite groups on the hill, then searching for a draft group. There was none in sight, so I started downhill alone, and just after the sharp turn, a group of speedsters came up on me and shouted, "Komm mit!" (Come with us!) I yelled back that I'd try, and I put all my effort into accelerating and latching into their draft—and I made it! They were fast. Faster than I was prepared for. But they were so cool and kept motivating me by cheering me on as I approached the lead position and then giving me a huge push from behind as I had to come in around the rear. This group taught me everything I needed to know about the art of rotating and drafting in the span of about 15 minutes! Thanks, Team Schwögler!

That lap had energized me! It was now almost 8am. Eighteen hours into the race with six to go. I was going to make it.

My eighth and final lap was at around 10:15; it was relatively uneventful, but no less fabulous than the others, giving me a total of about 130 kilometers (80 miles) on a glorious day. In the end, our team finished 45 laps together, an equivalent of 738 kilometers (460 miles) with about 20 minutes to go before the 24-hour mark, and placed 12th of 40 mixed teams.

All the teams stayed for the amazingly rowdy awards ceremony (how do these people still have so much energy?). Finally, at about 4pm, the fatigue settling in, we packed up our gear and wearily headed home and back to the reality of our lives.

CHAPTER 25

AN ANGEL IN FLIP-FLOPS

Sometimes we experience strange events, or encounter people who make a brief appearance in our lives and have a bizarre impact on us, though at that moment we can't quite understand its significance or meaning. When I was racing in my second Kelheim 24-hour bike race, I had just such an extraordinary encounter.

After reaching the peak of the initial monstrous climb to the Befreiungshalle, I found myself in a group with four men. We took the initial descent together and stayed close, drafting interchangeably on the flat to keep up speed and save energy. Then we passed a man on a bike who was apparently just out for an easy Sunday ride. Although he was on a slick race bike, he had no start number, no helmet, and no shoes. Ok, he had flip-flops on, if that counts. But he was clearly not part of the race.

Just after passing him there was a steep descent, and we were still tight in a pack. Next came the 90-degree curve, and as always I braked too much. I lost my group in the blink of an eye. But suddenly I felt a hand on my back and was given a huge push

The Befreiungshalle (Freedom Tower) over the city of Kelheim

from behind! Naturally I was completely surprised though didn't turn around for fear of losing my balance, and I immediately took advantage of the momentum by pedaling like a maniac. A second later, I was passed, by the flip-flop biker. He positioned in front of me and gestured for me to stay in tight. He then tucked down and increased pace. I was speechless at first and then yelled to him, "But you have no helmet! No shoes!" He didn't reply, just kept up an insane pace of over 60 km/h for the next three kilometers downhill. Subsequently, where the race course took another right turn onto the main road back into the city, the biker eased off, sat up in his seat, and without looking back at me, continued straight ahead on the small country road back up into the Bavarian hills. I took the right turn and headed back into town, wondering if I'd dreamed it.

Who would believe that story?

Probably no one. But I was pretty sure of one thing, though. I'd just had an encounter with an angel.

CHAPTER 26

A 65-KILOMETER WIN IN THE BAVARIAN FOREST

Let's get back to the year at hand. I'd finished the Marathon des Sables in April; in June I ran 100 kilometers in Biel; and now it was September and time for the annual Landkreislauf.

Given that I'd been on the waiting list for the Polar Circle Marathon since April and by September still hadn't heard a thing, I had all but written the polar circle off. Thus, the Regensburg Landkreislauf was planned to be the culmination of the year. (But as we all know now I still made it up to the Arctic before the year was out!)

It was the seventh year of the Landkreislauf, and I'd taken part in every one—the first four in relay teams and the last three as an ultrarunner. I was hoping to run it well, as the crowning of a fabulous year, since my training had been exceptional in preparation for the MdS. But what all athletes know is that an injury can sneak up on you at any time, and four days after Biel, while doing cartwheels with my kids in the yard, I tore my hamstring. For five long weeks I couldn't run. Though maybe it was a blessing in disguise as it gave my entire body time to recover from those two giant races, a break which I wouldn't have taken otherwise.

Training really started up again in full force during our family vacation in the United States in August. We spent two weeks out west, visiting Yellowstone National Park, Salt Lake City, and the Grand Canyon. I wasn't sure how many opportunities I'd have to run outside, but I did get some good runs in, with a few interval sessions and a long mountain trail run at Snowbasin outside of Salt Lake City. At altitudes of 6,000 to 9,000 feet, this was really good training. Then in Rhode Island I worked on endurance and mid-length tempo, and before I knew it the five weeks were over, and we were back in Germany. I was as ready as I could get.

The weather had been fabulous in the two weeks leading up to the race. Late summer, hot and sunny days with warm nights perfect for grilling and dinner on the terrace. But on the day of the Landkreislauf, the weather turned to fall: 14 degrees Celsius (57 °F) and pouring rain for the entire day. Instead of shorts and a short-sleeved top, I had to pull out my long compression socks, three-quarter tights, and a jacket.

In the two previous years, I was the first female finisher, meaning I was definitely feeling the pressure to make it a three-peat. There were 300 relay teams and 42 ultras registered, including five women ultras...and they were strong. Experienced ultrarunners and Iron(wo)men. Winning was not going to be easy. I would need a strategy. The distance was 65 kilometers (40 miles) with about 1,000 meters of positive elevation; the first 45 kilometers were relatively flat, and the last 20 kilometers heading into the

Bavarian hills were characterized by steep ascents and descents. That would be my only chance.

We all know by now that I don't like to run flats. I have trouble keeping up a pace for very long because I get bored, fall into a monotonous rhythm, and because the motion is not very dynamic, I start to stiffen up. So the plan was: Try to find a comfortable rhythm for the first 45 kilometers, stay as close as possible to the competition without losing too much ground, and then when I get into the hills where I feel strong, start to put the pressure on. But would it work?

I started the race near the front of the pack and was too fast over the first leg. I kept trying to slow down, but the flow of the other runners kept the tempo up. Finally, after 8 kilometers, I slowed down to where I wanted to be. Then at around kilometer 15, another female ultra passed me. I kept her in sight, so I wasn't too worried, but when the second woman caught me at kilometer 18, I wondered if I shouldn't try to pick it up. But the second runner and I decided to run together, and it was really enjoyable. We swapped stories and were entertained by my bike support, Nussi. He sang to us and relayed stories about how much the city had changed since he was a kid. The other ultrarunner was also a good pacemaker, and I was happy to just run alongside her and not have to pay much attention to my watch. Eventually the first female began to increase the distance between us, and by kilometer 35 the one by my side also began a slow break away from me. I hung back at a comfortable pace, knowing that there was a lot more to come.

It was still pouring rain, with occasional ferocious wind gusts, but thankfully, with my jacket (the trusty Salomon Fast Wing Hoodie that I had with me in the desert), I was not cold, though I was soaked to the bone. My shoes were squishy like sponges, and I felt hot spots forming on my toes and the balls of my feet. I knew blisters were on the prowl, but since they were not yet painful I tried to ignore them.

At about the 42-kilometer marathon mark, Frank was waiting with the kids and a friend of ours, Matthias, who would run with me for the rest of the race. Matthias was training for the Berlin Marathon, so this would be used as a long training run for him—and I was so happy to have the company and additional motivation!

Six minutes separated me from the lead woman, I was told. Then my start number ripped off my belt. The material was soaking wet and weak. I took off the belt and handed it to Nussi who tossed it in his gear basket. Matthias suggested we use his clip-style belt, which was in Frank's van. So after another flat four kilometers on a beautiful trail alongside a river, we saw our support vehicle and Matthias made the fix on the start number. Then into the woods for the first major ascent. The race was on.

Two steep uphill kilometers. I'd ridden it on the mountain bike two months earlier, so I knew what was to come. This time it didn't feel so bad. Or maybe I had just run it through my mind enough that it was no longer a mental threat. Either way, I was now in my element, and about halfway up the hill we caught up with the woman I'd been running with. She had slowed to a walk. As the climb steadied out a bit, she began to run again, and we were shortly together, but then on the next steep hill she slowed down again and that was the last I saw of her. One down, one to go.

Up, up, and up some more until we reached the convent in Frauenzell. That was where Frank told me that I had gained four minutes over the first female during the climb. Progress. But she was still nowhere in sight.

The course kept climbing and dropping. I pushed over the ascents and just let gravity take its course during the descents while concentrating on form and trying not to slip on the wet leaves. I was rejuvenated by the speed.

Over another ridge, across some fields, and down an embankment, and then she was in sight about 500 meters ahead. Still a huge distance. Matthias said, "We got her," but I said it was way too early and the distance was too great for an attack. There were about 10 kilometers (6 miles) remaining. I still had time.

We headed into the next patch of woods and suddenly we saw her stop and talk to two other ultras and a bike supporter. When I was about 100 meters away, they started to run again, but this time I knew it was only a matter of time. Back out into some fields, up another incline, and down the other side where the kids were shouting encouragement on my approach. They were so excited that I was back in the race and gaining ground. Nussi filled up the bottles, but I kept in motion.

There was another ascent before Brennberg, and I couldn't hold off the inevitable; I was consistently gaining. I soon caught two other male ultras and the bike supporter, and I knew that before we reached the top of that hill, the last major ascent, I needed to finally pass the lead female. I came up right behind her, then with all my reserves, I switched to the other side of the trail and powered by as strong as I could. She let out a deep breath. I kept up the pace upon entering Brennberg and soon heard screaming and shouting as Frank and the kids drove by me, thrilled to see that I'd taken the lead. I pushed with all I had until I was past the chapel, out of sight, and over the steepest point of the entire racecourse. This had cost me a lot of energy, but thankfully there were some descents ahead where I could get a shot of regeneration. I kept my strides long and my tempo high.

Going down a precipitous descent, I felt my quads beginning to burn, but there was no slowing down now. Before the next turn-off onto the trail into the woods, the van was again in sight, and my family was going crazy with cheers. That gave me more strength and determination to see the race through. Down, down, down until we were confronted with a steep uphill path that was a complete mud bath. Nussi had to dismount and walk. Even I, though unwillingly, had to slow to a march; the mud had cut my tempo so much so that it didn't make much difference in speed whether I walked or ran, and walking would reduce my heart rate.

Then into Dietersweg with a final onslaught of cheers from my family before they (and I) were headed to the finish. Only 4.7 kilometers to go. 4,700 meters. And mostly downhill. Still I never dropped the tempo.

With adrenaline pumping, that last kilometer was my fastest of the day. I could hear music and the moderator at the finish and knew it was almost over. One last look behind me to see if it was all clear, not yet aware that the next female was now almost a kilometer behind, and there was nothing left between me and the finish line. My three youngest kids came out to run the last 100 meters with me while Armin Wolf (my friend and moderator) announced my arrival. Emotions ranged all over the stratosphere. I have never been so happy to cross that line. I had gambled with my strategy, fought an incredible battle over 6 hours and

45 minutes through the worst of weather conditions, made my family and friends proud, and topped off the running season on the highest of highs.

That was my third Landkreislauf ultra. I had now won it three times in a row. I had my three-peat.

NOTES

Fluid Intake
- Water throughout the race, about 100 ml every 10 minutes, then alternating with oatmeal milk.
- Oatmeal milk starting at kilometer 43, about 50 ml every 20 minutes.
- Coke at kilometer 50—one sip and then did not want it again!
- Brought isotonic but didn't drink it.

Food
- Salted caramel GU (my favorite!) at kilometers 8, 18, 44, 50 (spit half of the last one out).
- One-third of a banana at kilometer 37.
- Salt tablets at kilometers 25, 44, and 50.

I did not stop to rest at all, but at kilometer 45, I had to prop my foot up for a second on the back of the van to scoop sand out of my shoe.

My first win in the Landkreislauf two years earlier...

A little history. The Regensburg Landkreislauf is a yearly event on the outskirts of the beautiful medieval city of Regensburg, and the course changes each time it is run. It is primarily a relay race, whereby teams of 10 battle over the same number of stages, each of differing length and difficulty. I'd run it every year since its inception in 2010, originally with a team of friends, and we called ourselves "5 Läufer & 5 Männer" (5 runners & 5 men). We were a just-for-fun group of friends, though in our second year we came in second place in the mixed division.

In 2014, I finally decided it was time for me to tackle all ten stages alone.

The official stats of my first solo start in the Regensburg Landkreislauf were 69.2 kilometers with 750 meters elevation for which I needed 7 hours, 17 minutes, and 32 seconds. I took a women's first place finish and was ninth overall. Naturally the numbers don't tell the whole story.

Driving to the start, we were greeted by raindrops on the windshield. The sky was varying shades of gray and would stay that way for most of the day.

A warm-up was not necessary. I'd get that in the first few kilometers which were all downhill. So I waited until about 30 minutes before the start to get out of my warm car and head toward the crowds. With a black start number, indicating that I was one of the 34 ultras, there were a lot of eyes on me. Video cameras were rolling, and photographers were milling about. I searched for anyone I knew, while my kids tried to stay close on my heels. I greeted our team founder, Armin Wolf, and his wife,

Alexandra, as well as my friend and occasional training partner, Felix, who was one of the relay starters.

"How about a quick interview?" asked the film cameraman working for our team. Oh, boy, here we go. "Ok," I replied with trepidation. Interviews in your mother tongue are tough enough, but in a foreign language when you are already at maximum nervousness? Just keep smiling.

Cheerleaders, music, announcements. The start was a blur, but suddenly I was running. After a kilometer I found myself with a rather large group of ultrarunners that stayed together for the entire first leg, making small talk and jokes as the sky drizzled down on us in a pine forest somewhere in the Bavarian hills.

By kilometer 15 our group had begun to separate, but I was still with three others, each of whom were running their first ultramarathon. One was on the phone making business calls, while the other was running exactly my tempo, and we were often in competition for the best side of the trail. Then finally I came around a corner and saw my nine-year-old daughter "on the lookout." She screamed to her sister, brother, and Frank that I was coming, and they scrambled to take photos and ask what I needed. Water bottles filled. A few gulps of oatmeal milk. Tuck another gel in the belt. And I was off again. Formula One pit crews would be envious.

At kilometer 23 I was met by my first "pacer." At the 6:00 min/km tempo that I had planned, my pacers were more there for motivational/entertainment purposes rather than to keep me at a certain speed, and I was thrilled that I had so many willing to help. Oliver (pacer 1) is a very talented runner on my team who grew up in the area we were running through, which is why he volunteered for that leg. As we ran through the village of Laaber, there was a very steep uphill section that we were forced to walk. We heard music and passed a house with tables set out front with beer, pretzels, and a hot grill. Oliver disappeared. A minute later he was back with an oversized pretzel in his hand and a huge chunk of it in his mouth, "Want some?" he asked. Uh, no, but thanks.

At kilometer 29 I saw my kids again in the distance and began waving. They immediately started running around, crazy with anticipation. Same routine. Filled the water bottles. Oatmeal milk. My daughter peeled a banana and held it for me as I took a couple of bites between sips of milk. A bite from a chia seed bar, then I was off again. Oliver said his goodbyes just before I came roaring into the next relay station where there was music, a moderator announcing my arrival, and fans watching me with amazed looks, high fives, and wild cheers.

I remember the very first Landkreislauf years earlier. I had run one leg on a relay team and was at the finisher's party as I watched in awe as several ultrarunners crossed the finish line. They had just run the whole course? I couldn't believe it. They were superheroes in my eyes. And now I was seeing those same looks in the fans who were lining the course…but this time their sight was focused on me! It was overwhelming, and each time it happened I got goosebumps. Still do.

At kilometer 50 I was met by my friend Carine and her husband Dejan who, along with their dog, would run the next 10 kilometers with me. Carine is French and her husband is Serbian, so they both have accents, as do I. So, imagine the scene…I've been running for five hours, I'm starting to get tired and really can't talk coherently anymore, at the same time my comprehension is wavering, so Carine and Dejan are trying to talk to me (in German, of course, a second language for all three of us), I'm understanding about half of it and simply grunting in response because they couldn't understand me anymore either; meanwhile the dog is still young and not yet fully trained so she's sniffing all around, sometimes crossing my path, with the leash winding around us. She is clearly not experienced at being with an ultrarunner nearing exhaustion, BUT the entertainment factor was just what I needed.

After a few kilometers, Frank and the kids met us again. With them were the kids of Dejan and Carine, and I remember looking at them and wanting to say hello but could not for the life of me remember their names although I've known them for years. This was the absolute lowest point in the race for me; we were at about kilometer 50, and I was more than ready to start drinking Coke. My legs were hurting, and the kids were all looking at me with really concerned (shocked) faces. I tried to smile, but don't think I was successful, so I figured it was best to keep moving. Dejan stayed with his kids at that point, so it was just Carine, the puppy, and me. We headed back into the woods and immediately onto some uphill trails. Carine is warm and bubbly with long curly auburn hair flowing freely as she runs. She was a super companion because she kept me completely distracted from any and all of the aches and pains slowly seeping into my body.

Frank met us again after about six kilometers. Water bottles were filled, and then Frank pointed in the distance and said, "Here comes the second woman." That was all I needed to hear, and I was off again, and this time alone. The next relay station had an out-and-back section leading into it. As I came out, I crossed paths with the woman right behind me—the gap was about 4 minutes, and there were 15 kilometers left in the race. I knew the woman behind me was a great runner, and I had no expectations of being ahead of her at all but, after 55 kilometers, there was no way I was going to lose this now, and I picked up the pace!

Shortly afterwards, a relatively steep descent confronted me, and I was practically in tears from the pain in my quads, which were throbbing with every downhill stride. But at the bottom of the hill my next pacer met me. Sonja, a half American–half German woman also from the running team, was waiting with Frank and the kids. This time I didn't even stop, just instructed Frank to give Sonja a water bottle, and she came running after me. Frank had briefed Sonja that I had a narrow lead and that if she could hold me to a 6-minute pace I'd probably keep it. She was nervous; she kept looking worriedly over at me. I sensed it too because she kept giving me words of encouragement. She is such a nice person and right from the start I apologized that I couldn't do much talking in response. I was happy to have her there, and she was carrying my water bottle, so I was perfectly content to simply follow in her footsteps; I didn't expect or desire more or less. A biker came up behind us, and after explaining I was a solo starter, he asked, "What kilometer are you on?" I looked at my watch, "62," I replied. The biker was dumbstruck and responded how I looked really good... considering. Uh, thanks. Perfect case of "looks can be deceiving."

We were then on another long, flat bike path along another stupid river! The second of the day. I was hating it. I kept looking off into the distance to get a glimpse of the bridge that brought me to the other side and back onto the trails, but it never seemed to come!

Sonja was amazing. She collected a can of Coke from her boyfriend who had zoomed up next to us in his car with my two youngest kids in tow. She returned, and I asked, a bit dumbfounded, "Was that two of my kids in the car with your boyfriend?" They had all just met each other less than an hour before and now they were racing around together. Yes, she replied with a laugh. "Boy, they sure make friends fast."

"Do you want Coke?" she asked.

"I don't know." I answered. She asked the same question again a few minutes later. "I don't know." I was exhausted. "I can't drink Coke from a can while running. And I don't want to stop anymore." Poor Sonja...what was she supposed to do? She said that she could mix it with the water in the squeeze bottle so that I could drink it on the go. "I don't know," was my reply. Then she was gone for a minute, and when she returned she handed me the squeeze bottle. Coke and water. I drank. Hmmm...not bad.

Frank was there again at the last checkpoint, but I didn't register much. I knew Sonja was taking care of me and that I only had about five kilometers to go. I just kept in motion. A few minutes later we were at the last relay station, and Birgit was waiting to join us. She had run earlier in the day on a relay team and had promised to join me for the finish. Now she was giving me some news about the race. Apparently, there was another ultrarunner not far ahead who looked like he was hurting. Was I *not?* You can catch him, she said. I laughed at that. That was the least of my worries.

A railway crossing was ahead of us. We were told by the organizers that we had to stop if the gates came down, or we could be disqualified. In the distance I could see that the gates were open. I picked up the pace and told the girls that I am not waiting for a train! Let's go! We got through and just a minute or so later we came across the other ultrarunner. He was walking, and we breezed by with words of encouragement. Then we needed to cross a semi-major road that had a pedestrian crossing light. The light was red for us, but there were volunteers working there to help control traffic for the runners, although apparently stopping traffic was not their job. So Birgit took over. She ran right into the street in front of a car and held up her hand for it to stop! I gladly hopped right across the street behind her. A short distance through a village, and then we came to a T-intersection at a horse corral. I'd run the course before and knew we had to go left there, but the girls, who were one step ahead of me, didn't know, and they both went to the right. I tried to tell them…left, left…but my voice was so weak they didn't hear, so I kept running and soon they came laughing back to my side.

Into the woods for a few more turns, and soon we came across one of the race organizers who was camped out there. I think he was calling ahead to the finish to let them know who was on the way in. Here I come!

Then came the last major hurdle—an infinitely steep incline of about 60 meters positive gain (or was it 600?) over a distance of about a half mile. I told Sonja I would walk. She replied, "You're not walking now!" It was agony. I suddenly heard whimpering coming from somewhere. Then realized it was me. Hang in there. "You're doing great!" Sonja called out from just ahead. No, I wasn't. She was not a good liar, but she was so supportive, and I was unbelievably grateful to have them with me.

Finally, I saw the top of the hill and the turn-off into the homestretch. It was essentially over, because at the top of that dreadful climb there was less than a kilometer left which cut gracefully downhill through a field and a small park. In the

With my kids just before crossing the finish line after 7 hours and 70 kilometers on my feet
© Gerhard Stuber

distance, I could hear the moderator and music at the finish, and I knew that my family, friends, and fans were waiting just behind the trees and across the overpass. I took off my shirt and handed it to Sonja; she offered me my team singlet to wear for the finish, but I didn't want it yet. This moment was for me. Feeling the cool breeze against my skin, I raised my arms like wings and "flew" down the hill, free as a bird. There was an indescribable exhilaration in knowing that I was about to finish this race, in first place at that, and all the hard work over the past months, the hours of long runs and the torturous interval training, flashed through my mind, for they were all worth it now, even if for just this one instant in time.

One year later at the start of my second Landkreislauf as an ultra runner...

A whopping 97 beats per minute. That was my pulse at the starting line. To put that into perspective, my normal resting pulse is 47 beats per minute. My adrenaline supply was on overload. I couldn't stand still—jumping up and down, bouncing back and forth, and letting out a shrill yell any time there was an announcement or, even, for no reason at all. There was absolutely no calm before the storm. It was like experiencing a caffeine overdose. *And why do people keep squeezing my thighs and asking if I'm ready?* I was ready. After a year of looking forward to this race since I'd crossed its finish line the year before, I couldn't wait to get started.

That year I ran with my good friend (and physical therapist), Matthias. It was to be his first ultra, and although he is a much faster runner than I am over the shorter distances, we figured it would be a good idea for him to run my pace, since starting an ultra too fast is a recipe for disaster. And anyhow, what could be better than a seven-hour run with friends on a beautiful Saturday morning (…noon…afternoon)?

Before the start with Matthias

Now I'll break it down into the essentials…

Course Stats

As I've mentioned, the course of the Regensburg Landkreislauf changes every year. One year it takes place north of the city, then in the east or west, but this year it was in the south…my turf, crossing quite of bit of my training grounds. Overall distance was 70.7 kilometers (44 miles) with about 500 meters (1600 feet) of positive elevation, which is actually pretty flat over that distance.

Nutrition

Here's an exact play-by-play of what I consumed during the race.

Beverages

* Water (continually from kilometer 5 to 50; total approximately 3.5 liters)
* Oatmeal milk and water 50/50 mix (kilometers 35-55; total approximately 2 liters)
* Coke and water 50/50 mix (worked last year!) (kilometers 50-70; total approximately 1.5 liters)

I had an isotonic drink on hand in case of cramping, but did *not* drink any.

Food

* Power gel (kilometer 11)
* Power gel (not really sure but I think about kilometer 18)
* Half of a banana (kilometer 20)
* Half of a sports bar (kilometer 24)
* Power gel (kilometer 28)
* Small handful of roasted cashews in soy sauce (about kilometer 30)
* Half of a banana (kilometer 40)
* Half of a sports bar (kilometer 50)
* Half of a sports bar (kilometer 60)

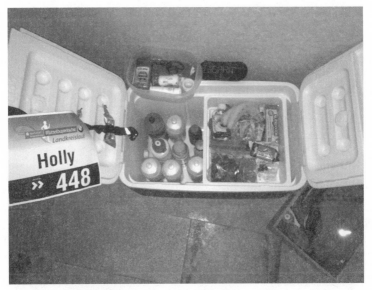

Packed and ready for the race

I know, that sounds like I didn't eat very much. It's true. I didn't, especially after kilometer 30. I planned to take in more calories, but somehow it didn't happen. Over the course of the race, I burned a few thousand calories and what I took in didn't come anywhere near to replenishing what was lost. But, I consider the oatmeal milk to be "food" as well as "beverage" as it supplies me with energy but doesn't tax my body via digestion to convert it. It's really a runner's superfood. *Check that?*

Now, the question is, how did I get access to this food? The first year my husband met me with the van at certain points where I would briefly stop and refuel, but this year it was planned a little differently.

This is where Nussi comes back into the story. Nussi is a good friend of Matthias. He accompanied us to carry our drink bottles, gels, sports bars, sunglasses, and whatever else we tossed at him. And, since that race, I haven't let him go, as he is my invaluable bike support each year for this event.

But, there was one catch. Nussi likes to talk. *A lot.*

Initially I was a bit worried about this. On the one hand, distraction and entertainment while running for seven hours is a good thing! But I was afraid I'd want to clobber him by kilometer 50. So, Nussi showed up at the start in a pink shirt. My favorite color. He said that he wanted to wear knee-length pink socks to match but that his wife wouldn't let him out of the house like that. Anyway, it turned out Nussi was a godsend—full of

Nussi, a.k.a. the Pink Panther

humor, entertaining us as well as the other runners, volunteers, and spectators. He thanked the volunteer firefighters stopping traffic along the course for sacrificing their "day off," and, most importantly, he was always making sure we got the food and beverage that we needed, when we needed it. He kept telling me I was the "blühende Leben" (literally translated as the "bloom of life;" but realistically interpreted as "Looking good!"). I mean, every time I looked at him—dressed in pink, carrying a loaded backpack on a pimped-up mountain bike with a granny basket on front—I couldn't help but smile!

Obviously Nussi couldn't carry all our drinks for the whole day, so my husband and kids, as well as Matthias' wife and daughter, all piled into our VW bus and met us at preplanned checkpoints along the course to resupply Nussi and give us motivation. It was so good to see that van in the distance…kids running wildly about, flags waving, stereo blasting, and the whole troop cheering us on as we approached.

Thus, with the help of four kids, two spouses, and the **pink panther**, we were nutritionally well supplied.

GEAR

Shoes

Backtrack to two weeks before the race, I'd bought a new pair of my favorite, tried-and-true trainers: the Mizuno Wave Inspire. For shorter distance road races, I use a lighter-weight shoe with less cushion (e.g., Saucony Fastwitch or Asics Gel) and for long-distance races with tougher terrain I typically wear an ultra-light trail shoe (e.g., Salomon S-Lab or the Inov-8 X-Talon) with less cushion but more grip on the sole. The Mizuno's were comfortable and would cushion me on the roads. Although, with my history of losing toenails, I'd bought them a half size larger and hoped that would be enough. They felt comfortable on the test runs leading up to the race, and I was confident I had the right shoe. In the end, the two baby toenails were unfortunately sacrificed, but that was still an improvement over the year before when I lost both of them plus one big toenail! Cha-ching!

Clothing

Temperatures were predicted to be around 20 degrees Celsius (68 °F) with little to no chance of rain, so I wore shorts, a short-sleeved shirt, and knee-length compression socks. I had extras of everything in the van, just in case, but only changed into my team shirt about one kilometer before crossing the finish line…after running for about two kilometers with no shirt on. *What?* I had a sports bra on, but the cool air felt so nice.

Safety Items

Also stashed in the VW "rescue" van I had: medical tape and gauze, isometric sports tape, Body Glide, safety pins, Compeed, Band-Aids, scissors, salt tablets, sun cap, sunscreen, etc. The only two items that I actually had on me in a small pocket in my shorts were my SPF-15 lip balm and my guardian angel which my friend had given to me before the Boston Marathon that spring. She still accompanies me occasionally when I think I may need her…the angel, not my girlfriend (unfortunately).

THE RACE

Well, to sum it up, we ran. And ran. And ran. Without stopping.

Ok, we power-walked a short steep section for about one minute at kilometer 37, and then I gave my husband a quick hug at kilometer 55. Other than that, we ran continuously.

The first 35 kilometers went by easy as a summer breeze. The weather was great, we cracked jokes, and a bunch of my running team members cheered me on as they were coming back toward us after having completed their own stage of the relay (doubling back to their parked cars at the start of their leg of the race). The person moderating through the transition zones kept us motivated; there they called out our names to the fans and waiting relay runners who dutifully cheered us on.

I knew my training hadn't been what it should have been for that distance, which isn't to say that I hadn't trained hard—six days a week with running, biking, and strength work—I was in excellent condition. But, due to vacation and family responsibilities, in preparation for this specific race I had only run three times over the 30-kilometer distance. When training for a normal marathon (42.2 kilometers), I usually run 30-plus kilometers at least **seven** times. *(Now I run that distance almost every Sunday. Is that how you identify a running addict?)* So, I knew that it would be a challenge, but I was confident that I could do it, since whether you make it to the finish line (barring an injury) is whether you have the high degree of mental stamina it requires. The body can endure amazing things if the brain tells it to.

Which is exactly what I was asking my body to do that day.

One problem with this relatively "easy" 70-kilometer, flat ultramarathon was the terrain. We were mostly on bike paths, fire roads through the woods, and tractor paths across fields, but a significant portion of those tractor paths had been recently covered with golf-ball sized loose rubble. This is difficult to run on at best and sheer agony when you've already got several dozen kilometers behind you. The last leg of the race was the worst in this regard and, in combination with the monotonous rhythm, putting one foot in front of the other over the last 8 kilometers was pure torture. Every cell in my body said stop! But my brain said, *you will only prolong your suffering if you stop and walk…just keep running until you cross that finish line…and then everything will be okay.* Another of my favorite mantras is to try to focus on the fact that, *running is one of my most favorite things in the world…what would I rather be doing?* There are not many things that rank higher for me.

Matthias began to pull away during those last few kilometers—or actually I dropped off the pace a bit. He slowed down and waited a couple of times, but I finally told Nussi to go ahead with Matthias; I'd be right behind them.

And then finally, at around 4pm, as I came out from behind a stretch of trees and looked across the fields, I caught a glimpse of the church bell tower in the village where the finish was. That's when I took off my shirt and just tried to appreciate the sensations that often go unnoticed: the cool air on my skin, the raw earthy smell of the freshly harvested fields, the remaining strength pulsing through my aching muscles, and the ground rolling away behind me under each footstep.

So, whether it was the mantras, the training, the support crew, or the sugar in the cola, I somehow made it across that finish line in 7 hours and 16 minutes, with two of my daughters at my side, Armin Wolf announcing my arrival to the crowd, and that enormous group of fans that give me goosebumps even now when I think about their uninhibited excitement at witnessing an ordinary person accomplish something extraordinary.

Finish line jump with my kids
© Gerhard Stuber

"Finished" at the finish

CHAPTER 27

WELCOME TO GREENLAND

At the beginning of October, I received an email saying that spots had become available for the Polar Circle Marathon, and they were now being offered to all competitors on the waiting list, where I'd been placed the week I returned from the Marathon des Sables that April. And since the marathon was in three weeks, I'd have to decide fast. Like, that day.

Of course, my first reaction was excitement, but then reality set in. We had just spent five weeks traveling in the United States, we were finally getting settled again into our routine at home, and I was slowing down into "off-season," not to mention that these race trips are not cheap. So I didn't really take it seriously. But I forwarded the email to my husband at work and his immediate reply was, "You have to do it."

What? Really? This surprised me a lot. I figured he would be hesitant like I was, but we'd talked about it back in April when I'd put myself on the waiting list, and he was happy that it came through. "It closes the circle," he said, which was true. From the Sahara Desert to the Arctic Circle.

I still wasn't convinced. I was sure that my kids would not be so enthusiastic, especially my youngest, at having me away again, so I decided I'd leave it up to them. That night at dinner I mentioned it, and the reaction was unanimous, "Mama, that is sooooo cool! You have to do it!" *What?* That was not what I had expected. This reaction was without doubt coming from the excitement that they experienced when I raced through the Moroccan desert. It gave me such positive reassurance that I'd made the right decision back then, not only for me, but also as a role model for my children.

So it was settled. I paid my fees, made flight reservations to Copenhagen, and booked a hotel there, which is where I would have to stay overnight on the way there and back, since the race package covered the trip from Copenhagen to Greenland and back.

Now what? Training? Too late to do much of anything different at that point, but since I'd just run an ultra two weeks earlier, my endurance was intact. Gear? At a predicted -10 degrees Celsius (14 °F) it wasn't extremely cold there; we have winter days here that approach that, and I go running then, so I didn't plan on buying anything new to wear. I already had winter chains for my running shoes, though I did get a pair of gaiters to keep any snow out. I just hoped we'd have a bright sunny day for the race instead of a snowstorm.

Now I just had to stay healthy and injury free, which isn't so easy in a house full of kids exposed to every virus in the Tristate Area (...*gotta love Phineas & Ferb*). As luck would have it, my kids all developed colds and were coughing as I was getting ready for the Limes Run which was two weeks before the Polar Circle Marathon.

The Limes Run is an extreme obstacle-course race, or mud run, in Bad Gögging, with a distance of 24 kilometers (15 miles) and 30-plus obstacles. The Armin Wolf Running Team was given five entries to the race. Let's just say I didn't initially jump at the opportunity to take part. I looked at the photos on the Internet from the previous years and saw people crawling through the mud, swimming in ice cold water, but, above all, I saw lots of smiling faces. So, due to the last observation, I agreed on one condition, that we would run in a group. I didn't want to have to go all out and battle the obstacles on my own (i.e., schlepp myself out of the mud pits); I just wanted to have fun, which is why most people take part in those races anyway. Although, there are a lot of athletes who won't run these races at all because of the high risk for injury or getting sick, but everyone has to weigh the odds and make their own personal choice. My philosophy is simple. Life is short. Try everything once. If you don't like it, you don't have to do it again. But you may be pleasantly surprised.

The weather had been cold the week before and even though the day of the race was expected to be much warmer, it was supposed to rain. So when I woke up that morning to gray skies I wasn't surprised; it wasn't till I started driving out to the race that I was amazed to see the sun come out and the clouds disappear! It stayed that way all day, sunny and mild temps…someone was smiling down on us.

There were three guys and two women in our group; Daniela (Dani) was the other woman, and she'd done a few of these before, although the last time she did one she seriously injured her knee and couldn't do any sports for almost a year, so getting through this race was mentally important for her. Christian, a physical trainer, and Dominik, a physical therapist, had done these before, and then there were Stephan and me who were virgin mud-runners, naïve but certainly not innocent.

We started in the fourth wave of runners, each wave separated by 10 minutes to avoid backups at the obstacles. After waiting half an hour, it was a relief to finally start, and the first kilometer was simply running through some fields to warm up. Then came the lake. A 150-meter swim in water temperature of 8 degrees Celsius (46 °F). When I got in the water, I could hardly breathe; my body was in shock. The rescue helpers were sitting in boats and yelling at us to take deep breaths. I just tried to get across as fast as I could, but as I was about halfway, I had caught up to some swimmers in front of me. I couldn't get around them, and they were kicking water into my face. I tried to stay calm and somehow managed to get across and out of the water. I was so relieved to have the swim behind me but was shocked to see a second smaller lake with about a 40-meter swim just in front of us followed by a mud pit! So, truth was, I wasn't really having fun yet. But that was just about to change.

We then ran along tractor paths through the fields and let the sun warm us. There were some beautiful Shetland cattle, and we decided to stop and take a group photo, as a friend was following us on his bike with camera. The five of us lined up, arm in arm, still soaking wet, where the only thing separating us from these mighty animals was a wire fence. An electric wire fence. As luck would have it Dominik's rear-end touched the metal wire and a shock wave ran through all five of us. We jumped with surprise then fell into hysterics when we realized what had happened—another photo with laughs, and we were back in motion.

Warning: Don't touch an electrified fence with your rear end when soaking wet.

© M. Seebauer

Outfits varied wildly: some in shorts and short-sleeved shirts while others were in long tights and multiple layers. A group of guys were dressed as Superman, red cape and all, while many were outfitted as Viking-type warriors.

Crawling through the mud on all fours, diving under canoes in the river, climbing up knotted ropes dangling from a bridge, and running through snow blowers, all of this was waiting for us, in addition to the total 24 kilometers of running and a whopping 14 times in the water.

Still it was fun, and after just under three hours we crossed the finish line with smiles on our faces and above all relief at having finished without any injuries!

Drafting behind Dominik through the snow blowers

But it's not over till the fat lady sings, and three days later I heard her bluesy tune as I began running a fever and had a sore throat and earache. The next three days were spent on the couch under a thick blanket; I was exhausted and totally stressed out about missing a critical interval session, but I had to get healthy or the Polar Circle Marathon would be out altogether.

A few days later, still weak but no longer feverish, I boarded a plane for Copenhagen. Arriving after dark, I needed to find a way to my hotel which was several kilometers from the airport, and since taxis are not cheap in the Danish capital, I decided to attempt using the local bus system. Now, anyone who knows me is aware that I don't use public transportation at all. Having grown up in a rural town in the United States, it is unfamiliar to me, and even after living in Europe for so long I've never warmed up to it. I decided to give it my best shot, though, and checked the schedules on the Internet and followed the signs in the airport for the bus terminals. Did I mention it was already dark? And why were there several bus stops in a row? Ok, just ask, right? So I approached the nearest bus and asked if he was going to Dragør. *Where?* he asked. Now, of course, I have no idea how to pronounce the minuscule (ø), so even after repeating myself I got a questionable look from the driver who then eventually understood (or was tired of trying) and pointed about 100 meters farther up the road to another stop. It was there that I saw the signs for bus number 35 and knew I was in the right place. Five minutes later the bus arrived, and all I had to do was make sure I got off at the right location…yep, in the dark. As luck would have it my stop was the terminal station, and from there I had a ten-minute walk to my hotel which I reached shortly after 10pm. I was exhausted, and sleep was easy to find.

At 7:00 the next morning, all participants were to meet in Terminal 2 of the Copenhagen airport for check-in. I chatted with a few other runners from Great Britain and the United States before boarding the Air Greenland flight for Kangerlussuaq—a five-hour flight, on which I had the best vegan airline meal ever: quinoa and zucchini, so amazingly spiced that I could have licked the tin tray clean. But I resisted.

Upon landing in Kangerlussuaq (roughly pronounced "Gan-ker-Schloo-Schooak"), we disembarked onto the tarmac and were greeted by clear skies and bitingly cold air. Since there was a four-hour time difference, and the flight was only five hours, local time was essentially only an hour after departure time in Copenhagen. Thus, it was 10am local time in Greenland, and of course our hotel rooms were not available yet. So, the tour group loaded us onto buses, and we drove out to the glacier to see where we'd be running on the weekend. The landscape was breathtaking. We saw caribou and even a pristinely white Arctic hare hopping through the snow. We stopped along the route for a lunch break where we were given sandwiches and could get out of the buses to enjoy the view. Eating a sandwich with a glove is not so easy, but without them my hands were quickly turning numb. Some of the shredded lettuce had fallen out of my roll into the container and froze instantaneously; I began to question why I was there. We were having mild weather and sunshine at home. I hate the cold.

We'd been told in our itinerary to wear warm winter clothes for this outing to check out the race course, so back at the airport I'd slipped my winter snowboarding pants on over my jeans, and I had my warm Timberland boots, a hat, gloves, and a buff. I was still cold, but not as cold as some of the others who only had on running shoes and jogging pants. This was probably due to the language barrier as all info was given to us in English. In fact, the group was full of more than twenty nationalities, and I heard so many different languages on the bus. There was a group from China, including a young woman in a flashy red mini-skirt, a fluffy short white jacket, and white high-heeled boots; she looked like Minnie Mouse, giggling and posing for photos. We all wondered if she was actually there to run or just entertain her friends and keep her boyfriend warm at night. There was also a group from Italy who all had on the same hats, striped with the colors of the Italian flag. They remained in a constant state of jubilation during the entire weekend, whether crossing the finish line, in the bar, or at breakfast after a few hours of sleep (I know this because their room was next to mine and the walls were thin). After nearly two hours driving on the snow-covered rolling terrain, the buses arrived at the glacier, which brings me to a good point. I think now is time for a short lesson in the geology, geography, and climate of Greenland (many thanks to Wikipedia).

Greenland is covered by the only permanent ice sheet outside of Antarctica. The average daily temperature of the capital city of Greenland, Nuuk, which lies on the southwest coast, varies throughout the year from -8 to 7 degrees Celsius (18-45 °F). The total area of Greenland is 2,166,086 km^2, of which the ice sheet covers nearly 80% with a volume of approximately 2,850,000 km^3, which is something like eight cubic meters of ice for everyone on the planet. That's a lot of margaritas! The highest point on Greenland is Gunnbjørn Fjeld at 3,700 meters, whereas the majority of Greenland is less than 1,500 meters in elevation.

Southern Greenland lives up to its name as agriculture thrives there with many farms, whereas the extreme north of Greenland, Peary Land, is not covered by an ice sheet, because the air there is too dry to produce snow, which is necessary for the production and maintenance of an ice sheet. If the Greenland ice sheet were to melt away completely, the world's sea level would rise by more than seven meters.

All that said, the important point here is that most towns and settlements of Greenland are situated along the ice-free coast, with the population being concentrated along the west coast. So nearly the entire coastline is free of ice, but you only have to drive a short way inland from any of the cities to reach the ice cap.

The main outpost for the Polar Circle Marathon is right there at the airport hotel in Kangerlussuaq, the only inland city in the country, which is accessible from the coast by a long fjord. From the "downtown" area where 500 residents make their homes, the ice cap is only about 30 kilometers (19 miles) away, accessible along the "longest road in Greenland." Seriously. The 30-kilometer mostly gravel road connects Kangerlussuaq with the Russel Glacier and the ice cap and was built by the American occupation after the Second World War. The road was then reinforced by a company which oversees winter automobile tests, though it is no longer used for that purpose. Other than that, cities in Greenland are only accessible to each other by water or air.

The Russel Glacier

Surely the planners and developers of this road for car testing had absolutely no vision that the future of this road would also be suitably purposed for running a marathon.

The majority of the Polar Circle Marathon is run on this road, with the start of the race near the very end of it at the glacier, sending us initially in the direction of the glacier and onto a 5-kilometer loop directly on the ice cap, then back onto the snow-covered gravel road for a jog back to town.

So, back in the bus. We'd arrived at the end of the road and were guided over a stony promontory and onto a section of the marathon course. It was magnificent. A massive presence of ice and snow, very distinctive when compared to land, not flat but with many undulations and tinged a light blue. The adjacent landmass was characterized with strewn rocks and many small hills, whereas the glacier rose high and was purer in color.

The course tour two days before the race

The glacier, also sometimes referred to as the ice cap, was amazingly beautiful, so I kept my iPhone in hand for photos. Of course, I had to remove my glove each time I wanted to take a photo, but it was worth it. Until my phone suddenly went dark. It was too damn cold. The temperature outside was about -14 degrees Celsius (6 °F). No matter what I tried, the phone did not work again until I got back to the hotel, plugged it in, and had to restart it.

The ride back to the hotel was relatively monotonous as we were all really tired, we were driving back along the same road we'd already seen, and we were anxious to get settled into our rooms. Once we were back at the hotel and were finally given our room assignments, I was pleased to find myself sharing space with a 52-year-old Norwegian woman who was not picky as to which side of the bed she should sleep on. We got along really well from the start, and after resting for a bit we went to the bar for a beer

Which way to Oz?

before dinner—55 Danish crowns for a 0.33-liter beer, equal to 7.50 Euro or about $8. This may be normal around the world, but coming from Bavaria with the highest density of breweries in the world and the price of a half-liter (!) of beer at around 3.50 Euro, the prices there were outrageous…but one must consider the transport costs and the view. Ok, the view was not so great, looking over the airport runway, but still, we were at the end of the earth, and that counts for something.

As our hotel was part of the airport facility, we ate breakfast and lunch in the cafeteria there, but for dinner they had an excellent restaurant. My expectations were not very high that I'd get any vegan food while there, but with four other vegans on the trip as well as several vegetarians, we were treated with some delicious meals.

The following day gave us time to acclimate. I had booked a tour of the "City and Tundra." I figured the city tour would take about five minutes on foot, but they actually packed us into yellow school buses (unheated), and we drove out to the harbor at the tip of the fjord. "Harbor" is a bit of an overstatement, but there was a giant cement docking area and even a large vessel with a backhoe on board that was busy dredging the harbor of sand that washes down during the spring and summer from the glacial melt. Apparently, there is so much of the sand that when mixed with the full force of the melt water it creates a massive force which even washed out a bridge a couple years earlier. During the summer months small cruise ships come to dock there; the passengers disembark for a day trip to the glacier. But now it was deserted except for the backhoe operator. Crystalized ice was floating on the water surface. Winter was on its way.

We were told that out of the 500-person population in Kangerlussuaq, 150 of them were children. They had a school, playgrounds, an ice rink, and even a swimming pool. There was no farming or other production industry, so the entire workforce was employed at the airport, hotel, or somehow tied in with the tourist industry by owning small handicraft shops or offering tours.

We passed by the cemetery which had only two souls buried in it. This was because it was a relatively new city. It was built by the Americans during the Second World War, who remained there until 1992. So it's only been in the hands of the Greenlanders for a quarter of a century, and as most Greenlanders are traditionally buried in the city where they are born, no one who had been born in Kangerlussuaq has yet died.

The airport is sheltered by two mountain ridges on either side, which allows for safe aircraft landings in almost any weather. Our school bus chugged up to the top of one of the ridges where we had a spectacular view of the barren tundra beyond. There were rolling plains of ice and snow as far as you could see. I was sure the only thing green in Greenland at that moment was my jacket. In the distance we saw several dark figures that our tour guide assured us were grazing musk oxen, and even though they occasionally moved, without binoculars we couldn't be sure what we were looking at. A couple of caribou were lying on a hillside. An intermittent large crow circled overhead.

It was excruciatingly cold on top of the mountain. We couldn't stay outside of the bus for long, and even sitting inside the vehicle provided little respite. But we tried to make the best of it and made jokes and small talk among ourselves.

Bits and pieces of our lives would be revealed over those few days; we came from all walks of life. There was a man from Los Angeles who was a caricaturist for Disney, recently drawing for

Frozen among other films; we sat enthralled as he told us behind-the-scenes stories from the entertainment conglomerate, which movies we can expect sequels from and which were retired. A man who'd recently had some type of business book published was having photos taken of him with his paperback against the backdrop of the glacier and frozen tundra. There was a high-ranking UN official who travelled the world, running ultras. A jovial French woman was there to run her first half marathon (both the full and half marathon distances were offered...several did both since they were on succeeding days), and after having drunk us under the table at the bar each night, you'd never guess she had a PhD in mechanical engineering from MIT and was in charge of the turbines and crew on an oil rig off the African coast. An American diplomat living in Syria had me laughing so hard I was reduced to tears when she recalled how bodyguards were required to accompany her on her training runs. They initially tried to run with her, but when they realized she sometimes ran for hours on end, they began following her in a car, conveniently carrying her water bottles as an added benefit. Suprisingly, many people were there to run their very first full or half marathon. A quirky German chemist was there to run his last. *Why come to the end of the world for your first big race? Why not try something easier close to home to start off with?* These people not only had the love of running as a common thread, but also the love of adventure.

Back down into the city, we made our last stop at the sled-dog kennels. I'd been to a dog-sled lodge in northern Sweden and experienced how the dogs were lovingly raised and cared for, but here the kennels gave me the impression of a doggie death camp. There was simply a compound of cages set onto a promontory on the fjord; there was no adjacent home with an owner, not even a hut with a caretaker, just mangy wild dogs, slightly curious but fearful at our presence. In one of the cages that I approached there lay the remains of a giant raven on the ground that had been mutilated and pulled apart. One of the dogs was gnawing on a wing. Between the cages a large mass of frozen fur and flesh could be seen half covered in snow. A large box of bones. Caribou skull and antlers. I got back in the bus.

That afternoon I took a short test run to make sure I was confident with my clothing and gear. The temperature was a balmy -7 degrees Celsius (19 °F) with bright sunshine. I was sweating in three layers. Clothing adequate: check. I'd brought my sand-proof goggles that I'd had with me in the Sahara and thought they might be good to protect my face from the cold and provide vision during a snowstorm, but for some reason they kept fogging up on the test run, and I decided to leave them home the next day. I ran with my YaxTrax spikes on, and they felt good. Many runners planned to use spikes only while on the glacier and then remove them for the remainder of the run on the snowy gravel road, but I find them so easy to run in, giving me more confidence with each step on an ice- or snow-covered surface, so I anticipated using them during the entire race. But just to be sure, I took them off and tried running without. It was slippery. A decision made simple.

After a shower with still some time before dinner, my roommate and I decided to check out the grocery store across from the hotel, the only one in town, to see what kind of local delicacies they might have. We looked for whale or seal meat. They had none. I was slightly relieved. The few gift shops next door were closed, so we simply looked in windows and saw lots of handicrafts made of seal skin and oxen hair.

There was an obligatory race briefing prior to dinner. Then into the restaurant to tank up on carbs. But although the chef could whip up delicious meals, he was clearly not an endurance athlete as the vegans were served a dinner of warm hummus, chickpeas, and cabbage. Absolutely delicious, but packed with protein and blatantly lacking carbohydrates. Not like my traditional pre-race meal at home of my homemade potato soup and a spinach salad! Couldn't even top it off with a carb-loaded beer as alcohol affects the nervous system for 24 hours. Argh!

It would have to do. I knew I wouldn't be pushing the limit the next day anyway, but I'd have to be careful to take my gels at regular intervals to keep my blood-sugar level up. Just hope the gels don't freeze.

Back up in the hotel room, I laid out all the clothes I'd have to pile on for the marathon the next morning and made one last check of my drop bag. It was only 8pm, but I was jet-lagged and exhausted. Time for bed.

CHAPTER 28

THE POLAR CIRCLE MARATHON

I was awake at 3:45am. No need for an alarm. I scrolled through my messages on my cell phone. Checked the news and weather.

Breakfast started at 5:30am and that was when my roommate and I were more than ready to get down to the cafeteria. Two pieces of toast with margarine and jelly, oatmeal, and tea. Then back upstairs to get dressed under multiple layers, much too much clothing for anything ordinary.

The buses taking us to the starting line were supposed to leave at 7:00, but it was 7:20 before we finally got underway. It was still dark. "Bus" is just a general description for the vehicle we were transported in, because what we were actually traveling in were windowed containers with seats, which were set upon the bed of a big-rig capable of traveling through deep snow and up and down steep hills. The tires even had small spikes built into them to increase traction. The vehicles were really functional in this environment, but there was also a downside—sitting in the back we were isolated from the driver. He couldn't see or hear us, and although we'd been given a two-way radio the previous day on our tour to the glacier, the morning of the race we had no radio and were essentially cutoff. Twice along the trip to the starting line the caravan of buses stopped, and we saw runners in the buses ahead climbing out to empty their bladders of the morning coffee, but we had no way of telling the driver to let us out, too, and we were locked inside. Thank goodness none of us were desperate.

The Arctic bus

After about 90 minutes we arrived at the start and were told we should stay in the bus till the starting line was ready because it was extremely cold and windy. But by now everyone in our bus needed a potty break. So we were told to go do our business and then get back into the bus to wait for the start. As our bus emptied and the bitter cold and brutal winds hit us, I saw some of the women run up the road to go drop their drawers hidden behind a large rock. What were they thinking? This was not a time to be shameful. My roommate and I simply ran behind the bus and pulled down our leggings, struggling to get them back up and in place before we climbed back into the vehicle. I think I must now hold the world speed record for pulling up compression tights. The ferocity of the wind was an

Spiked tires

unwelcome surprise. The weather forecast was for little to no wind on race day, but it had been wrong. The extreme cold and gusts were a shock to the system. A temperature of -17 degrees Celsius (1 °F), with gale force wind. Wind chill at least -25 degrees Celsius (-13 °F). Good God.

Back in the bus for the final minutes, and the anticipation was killing me, as well as everyone else. No one was sitting down. Everyone was crammed in the aisles, like bulls waiting for the gate to drop. Finally we got the word that the start would be in three or four minutes, and the starting line was about 50 meters from our bus, but before going there we still needed to drop our bags on the large green tarp so that our gear could be returned to the finish line. We didn't have much time. But why was no one getting off the bus? After a minute or so, those of us in the back started to lose patience and wanted to get out, but the Chinese group in the front were blocking the door and didn't look like they were in a hurry to go anywhere. So I started with a few rousing hoots and team calls, "Let's get this show on the road!" The others in the back followed suit and started cheering, which got things going and soon we were finally out. I was immediately blasted by the wind. I pulled my windbreaker out of my pocket, which was supposed to be for emergencies. I promptly deemed the situation an emergency. I put it on and never took it off. There were men holding the poles on each side of the starting banner spanning the road, otherwise it would have blown away. It was like a dramatic rescue operation. I felt like we should be hurrying for shelter, helping the wounded, not standing at the starting line of a race. It was completely crazy. I was in the front row to start because I wanted to be in the photos. What? Why not? The starting line photos are always cool, and I'm never in the front row, usually the second or third, hidden behind the tallest guys in the race. But today I wasn't shy, and I elbowed a couple of people to hold my place in front.

My sunglasses were on even though the sun was not up, just to protect my face. In that same vein, that morning I had smeared myself so much with Body Glide that I could have gone to film a porno instead of run a race. But protecting any exposed skin was critical to avoid frostbite.

Then the race director was screaming a countdown which could only be heard by the few people who were directly in front of him before the wind carried his voice away, but that was enough to get the group started. 3...2...1...and we were off. The first steps rolled smoothly and felt good. But why was everyone still behind me? Normally I am practically steamrolled by the pack, but this time I was the leader for about the first 50 meters, until the guys finally started to find their pace and bust past me. I didn't care whether I was too fast, I just wanted to get going and warm up.

We started uphill on a road that had a couple of tracks from a four-wheel-drive vehicle that had gone through earlier, but the ruts still had deep snow, and it was really hard to run. The wind was ferocious, and we crossed a pass where it blew through like a wind tunnel. I felt like I was running in place, literally standing still. It reminded me of trying to move against the forces of the snow blowers during the Limes Mud Run two weeks before. Ice crystals battered my face and bit into my skin; I futilely tried to shield myself with my hands.

My toes were so cold after the first kilometer that I thought for sure I would end up with frostbite. I kept trying to wiggle them, but it got harder and harder to get them to move. I started to get scared. I knew that personally I could live with having to have a toe amputated, but I was actually afraid of what my children would think of it and if it would embarrass them.

Then at kilometer 2 there were two race organizers stopping us and checking our faces for signs of frostbite. I heard after the race that there were several people who were pulled out at that point because they were showing initial signs of exposure on their chins and cheeks. They were brought into the all-terrain vehicle there, warmed-up, and treated before being rereleased onto the course.

I told the helpers that my face was fine, but my toes were cold. They checked my face and offered me one of the cups of warm elderflower drink. When I reached for the hot drink, a guy stepped on the back of my foot, and my shoe came off! I was so mad because this guy had been drafting off me for a while, which would have been okay, but he was running right behind me, too close, and now this. My feet were so cold already, I was scared I was developing frostbite, and now my shoe was off under my gaiter! I let him know that I was not happy with him. He must have seen the devil in my eyes because he then apologized about a dozen times.

Back on the run and off onto the steep rocky incline to access the ice sheet which covers 80% of beautiful Greenland. It really is a sheet of ice. Sections of it were almost like an upside-down egg carton of sheer bulbous ice. There was snow between the undulations, and you had to try to stay on the snow so you didn't slip, even with the spikes on. There was glowing ice as far as the eye can see, but in strange formations. Sometimes the snow was deep to my knees, other times it was completely blown free from the ice, and you had to carefully scurry across, though once I had to squat down and slide because it was steep downhill, and I was afraid that I would slip and fall. There were only about 20 runners ahead of me, and since the snow had completely blown over the course during the night, we were trail-breaking. The path was marked with poles at various intervals, sometimes with a piece of fabric at the top acting as a makeshift flag, dancing in the raging gusts. Just like in the desert, the path that you ran was of your own choice, as there was no trail in place; the poles were basically there for guidance and to keep you from getting lost. You simply had to navigate the terrain as best you could.

Although I'd never been in an environment like that before in my life, it reminded me of so many places I'd been—the sand dunes in the desert were similar in that the snow was slightly crusted on top and there were places that I could balance on it and not break through. Otherwise you just had to step in the footprints of those who had gone before you. But it was also like a technical trail run in the mountains, up and down, back and forth, in a jagged pattern with every step on uneven ground.

The wind was so strong that I absolutely had to keep my sunglasses on for protection, but it was a shame because the sun was not up, the light was dim, and I couldn't fully appreciate the true colors and beauty of the ice through the filter of my glasses. As I came upon the highest point in the course I was confronted with the most beautiful sunrise I'd ever witnessed. The color palette was breathtaking, the way the light reflected and played off the ice and snow was surreal. A bright pink sky illuminated the blue ice that extended to eternity. I felt like I must be very close to Heaven.

When running near the edges of the glacier, there were sections where it just ended suddenly, no transition. It simply dropped off several meters, and then there was earth.

Once I was finally off the ice sheet and back onto the deeply snow-covered road, I took a quick check of my watch to see how far I'd run and the time. I was shocked to see that it had taken me an hour to run only 7 kilometers. I felt like I'd just started, though my legs were already feeling the effects of having battled through knee-deep snow. Only 35 kilometers to go. But from there it was supposedly "all downhill" to the finish. Actually, the course was very hilly, with 850 meters of positive elevation and 1100 meters loss. So, in truth, we were running more downhill than up, but the rolling characteristic of the terrain made you feel like you were always about to face your next climb.

The road was good in some places where the vehicles had packed the surface, but in others the wind had blown snow over the route, and the tracks were narrow and deep. I was happy to have my gaiters on to keep the snow out of my shoes, but my toes were still cold. I kept trying to wiggle them around to increase blood flow, but it felt like I had stones in the front of my shoes in place of my toes. The rest of my body was warm enough, almost too warm when running uphill in the sun. I briefly considered taking off my light windproof jacket (yes, the same one from the desert and the Landkreislauf), but I was not uncomfortable, and as I've learned when running ultras…don't change anything unless it is necessary or unavoidable.

Just coming off the glacier at the Polar Circle Marathon
© www.Marathon-Photos.com

I stopped at all the aid stations to drink and chatted briefly with the helpers. Those poor souls were freezing. At least I was moving and keeping warm, but they were there serving us in the most extreme environment imaginable, so the least I could do was stop and greet and ask how *they* were doing. Every five kilometers they served cold (and sometimes icy) water and a warm beverage: either a warm elderflower or warm isotonic drink. Once they also had sports bars available, which I needed help opening because my fingers were just too cold to grip properly. You absolutely had to stay there to drink because there was only one cup allotted per runner due to environmental awareness. Of course, you could fill your cup as many times as you wanted, stand there and drink, and then dispose your cup in the garbage bag. But at those icy temperatures I did not feel thirsty, so during the first 15 kilometers at each aid station I drank only a small cup of water, but by about kilometer 20 I noticed that I was feeling really drained, so I trouble-shooted the problem: Speed too fast? No. Enough energy via food? Yes. Mineral deficit? No. Dressed properly? Yes. Pain anywhere? No. My body was numb. Enough fluids? Oops.

At the next aid station at kilometer 21, I drank two full cups of water and two of the elderflower drink. I soon felt better, but still pretty drained after the intensity of the first hour of running over the ice sheet.

After passing the half marathon mark, the rest of the course became relatively monotonous—up and down, still cold, beautiful scenery—but I was really ready to find the finish line. There were, for obvious reasons, no spectators along the course. A couple of runners passed me between kilometers 15 and 25, including a woman who'd removed her gloves and was taking off her jacket while explaining that she was going through menopause and was always too warm. Then there was a Swiss runner who withdrew his Go-Pro camera from a pocket and filmed us running side by side before he increased his pace and slowly disappeared over the next hill. But during the last 15 kilometers I found myself passing a few runners who'd slowed their pace, some to a walk, as is common in any marathon. The refreshment station at about the 30-kilometer mark was where I stopped to eat a granola bar, but my fingers were too numb to open the package, so the race helper had to do it for me. That was when I noticed a female runner coming up from behind; she seemed very eager to overtake me and only stopped for a brief moment to somewhat spastically suck down a gulp of water before hurriedly getting on her way again. I had no ambitions for this race and knew I wouldn't make it on the podium anyway, so I let her go, unconcerned. As I began running again, she kept turning around to see if I was gaining on her. This entertained me for a while as I'd sometimes even take the outside of a curve so that I'd still be in sight. Didn't want her to think she was leaving me in the dust!

The kilometers were all marked along the course, which provided a small token of motivation by breaking the war down into battles. Although, it was a little disheartening when, by the time I got to the 41-kilometer mark, I still couldn't see the finish line, though the woman in front of me remained clear in my sights. But just afterwards, I crested a hill and saw the airport, my hotel, and just beyond that was the point at which I could stop running. There were a few runners who'd already finished and were cheering as I approached. When, after 5:03.09, I crossed the finish line in 6th place, a woman put a medal over my head and also gave me a welcoming hug. I'd never experienced this before at a finish line—a hug—but it was so wonderful. It was a gesture of praise, and I was so completely empty it just made me want to melt into her arms, as if she were my mother who would then carry me home. But, reality check, I needed to get into some warm clothes, so I collected my winter jacket, some food, and then hurried back to my hotel room for a hot shower!

As I undressed and took off my shoes, I noticed that my right sock was bloody on one side. This was not surprising after a marathon, but naturally not entirely welcome. So I hesitantly took off my sock to find….nothing! No cut. No blister (on that foot). And nothing that appeared to have caused some bleeding. An unsolved mystery. On the left foot, though, I had severe pain under the second toenail, and I had to take a safety pin underneath the nail to pop and drain a blood blister. Ouch. And, unfortunately, even after a hot shower, my big toes were still numb.

After I showered, warpped my hair up in a towel, I watched out the window as runners kept coming in, which I could do easily because the hotel was right on the race course. Each time I saw someone I knew, I'd open the window for a quick moment to cheer them on.

We celebrated with the whole group that night. As we relayed our stories, we laughed ourselves into hysterics, partly due to the exhaustion, partly from the wine and beer. We named our small group the "Chilled Team." One of the women mentioned how a crazy lady with a towel on her head was screaming at her out of the hotel window as she was approaching the finish line. *Really? Some people are nuts.* Late into the night we were all rewarded with a show put on by Mother Nature: the Northern Lights.

It wasn't until I was in bed later that night, recalling the events of the day, with the satisfaction and peace of mind of again having accomplished something extraordinary, that I realized I'd finally regained sensation in all my toes. I immediately felt relief for the sake of my children that I wouldn't have to amputate any appendages due to frostbite.

A good sign. I could keep running ultras. At least for a while…

CHAPTER 29

LOCKED NAKED IN A CAGE

When I first started running races, I had gotten myself into a pre-race routine, as most people do, which not only included tapering the training but also modifying my diet, as well as no alcohol for at least several days beforehand (ok, at least one day beforehand). At the time I was an everything-eater—meat, dairy, sweets, alcohol—there were no limits. But once I'd started to run more I noticed the difference what I ate made on my ability to run "fast." I had gotten into the habit of eating no meat for about a week before a race and significantly reducing my dairy intake. This just made me feel lighter, quicker, and more energetic. But as soon as the race was over I would go back to the old conventions, until I came across a book by the one of the kings of ultrarunning, Scott Jurek, called *Eat & Run*.

Living in Bavaria, Germany, since 2000, I am not up on all that is going on in the United States and hadn't heard of Scott Jurek until I read the book *Born to Run*, which was given to me as a gift by a friend living in the States. So when I came across his name, highlighted by notoriety, I looked him up and found out that he had written his own book, the subtitle of which was really why I bought it: *My Unlikely Journey to Ultramarathon Greatness.* I'd always been intrigued by ultramarathons and thought it might be a good read, give me some inspiration, and help me prepare for my upcoming marathon. It wasn't until I'd started reading that I noticed the recurring theme and realized that the guy was a vegan fanatic. I am almost ashamed to admit it, but until that point I hadn't even heard the term "vegan" before. Or if I had, I hadn't given it a second thought, considering it simply to be some kind of extremist form of vegetarianism that wouldn't interest me in the least.

But after seeing what this guy could achieve when living on a plant-based diet, I began to question my own eating habits. If cutting out meat and dairy helps me in races and makes me feel better in general, then why do I only do that before races and not all the time? So, I decided to give it a try. I had six months before my first marathon, the Berlin Marathon, so I thought I would go vegan until then, leaving the option open afterwards to return to old habits.

Though you have to understand something—veganism was really unheard of at the time in Germany outside of the major cities. And when I say "at that time," I don't mean decades ago; this was in 2012. There were no books, no cookbooks, no vegan substitutes in the supermarket, and if a restaurant had even a vegetarian option on the menu, then it was really considered forward thinking. Vegan meals could not be found anywhere outside of my home.

When I moved to Bavaria, I was overwhelmed by the wurst, or sausage, consumption. There was not only bratwurst, but also gelbwurst (like bologna), blutwurst (blood sausage), and infinite selections of local specialties. At first, I was open to trying everything in my new home and adapted culture, but I can remember at one point during my first year living here and sitting in a beer garden for dinner. I was not in the mood for meat and just wanted to order a salad. There was not even a small, green house salad on the menu, but there was a "Wurstsalat," a sausage salad. So, still new to the area and not speaking great German at the time, I figured I'd order the salad, eat the veggies, and just pick the wurst out of it. Wrong. The "salad" was comprised completely of half-dollar-sized gelbwurst discs, drowned in vinegar, and smothered in onions. *Sigh.*

So, other than when eating out, I went vegan with really no trouble at all. I did not crave meat and was thrilled with having left my digestive troubles behind me. I'd struggled with constipation for years, and it had all but disappeared overnight. Lactose intolerance is a strong likelihood, but no need to go back there to test it out. I still cooked meat for the rest of my family, sometimes preparing two completely different meals, but usually I compromised by making vegan side dishes that we all ate. It wasn't too long, though, before my husband started to prefer my meals over the meat dishes, and then two of my daughters jumped on the bandwagon. So more often than not we eat vegan, and if my younger kids want meat, then I simply cook that as a "side dish."

Most people believed I was nuts. They thought I was going overboard with the fitness craze. Though I did not advertise my decision, upon finding out, some people would even challenge me on it. Once when I was snowboarding, we sat with a group in the lodge for lunch, and while everyone was ordering Schnitzel and french fries, I pulled out my bag lunch and was quietly eating my veggie wrap. Someone next to me asked if I was vegetarian, and

I quietly replied, "Actually, I'm vegan." A man across the table heard the exchange and jumped right in. He began asking me why I thought humans were given teeth if we weren't supposed to eat meat and that our species has survived for millennia so why do I think I know better? Despite the fact that there are scientific studies proving that animal protein is harmful to our health, I honestly don't feel like I need to justify my stance to anyone, let alone a stranger. I choose not to eat meat. It is right for me. I don't force my opinions on anyone else, but if someone politely asks why I do it, then I tell them. Some immediately look to my shoes or belt and ask, Then why are you wearing leather? That cost an animal its life, too! *Are you not listening to me? I do it for my own health benefits, not to save Bambi.* Although I love animals, I am not an animal activist and probably never will be.

Ok, that's not exactly true. I was an animal activist, briefly, for about eight minutes, while locked outside in a cage, naked, on a freezing cold December morning in Munich on the Oktoberfest Fairgrounds.

Let's just let this cat out of the bag. It was a type of protest event entitled, "Die Krönung der Schöpfung," loosely translated as "The Crowning of Creation." The idea came from performance artist Wolfgang Flatz, who designed a three-storied café-style cage to hold activists taking a stand against industrial livestock farming. The cage was large enough to hold several hundred people, but considering the circumstances—early Saturday morning, temperatures hovering at the freezing point, no clothing allowed—well, only 63 people showed up. And I was one of them. I just thought it was a really cool idea, and I cajoled my girlfriend Stephanie to go down there with me. She was heavily hungover, or actually still a bit drunk at the time, so cold temps did her good to get back onto the path to sobriety.

It was a cool event, in more ways than one, and though we were on the public fairgrounds, it was cordoned off that morning to keep voyeurs at bay. The event was professionally photographed and published in newspapers and online. You can look it up on the Internet, since I am not including photos here. I'm in the middle level of the cage, whereby we are all standing, and I am shrewdly crossing my legs for a bit of privacy. And I'm sure lots of unofficial photos made the social media rounds that day, too, as the medical and security crews on hand were semi-secretively snapping photos from their cell phones the whole time.

Unfortunately, since we were only several dozen people instead of several hundred packed uncomfortably inside the cages, the photos were not exactly reminiscent of the horrible images we see of animal handling, so the cause was not likely to have been convincingly supported by the event. But it was definitely memorable for Stephanie—who is actually a model mother, wife, and friend—and me. And though she and I are close friends, and despite all the "normal" and "well-behaved" things we've done together, it's amazing that her only appearance in this book is a drunk and naked public display.

But I digress once again.

Eating a plant-based diet has now become routine. I don't particularly like meat substitutes, such as soy-based burgers or sausages, so I have learned to be creative with vegetables, legumes, and grains. I try to maintain a basic rule of color variation on my plate, at least three colors, and then I know my vitamins are sufficient. I love what I eat. It makes me feel good. That's enough for me. And that's all that matters.

CHAPTER 30

THE FINISH LINE

Not long ago, when I was running near my home in Germany, I paused at a fence to stretch, and there was a man in the driveway adjacent who spoke to me, asking, "Are you Holly Zimmermann? Famous from radio and television?"

I had to give it my best effort not to laugh. He was being serious. But something like that had never happened to me before. It was so Hollywood-esque. And it made me feel good. (P.S. I am not famous.)

American friendliness is legendary. Many Europeans think we Americans are superficial. I can understand why they think that. I've lived in Germany for many years, and it took me a long time to not only learn the language but also to understand the people and their ways, and I am now forever grateful for having the chance to live completely immersed in two distinct cultures. Conversely, when I first moved to Germany, I wondered why everyone was so cold and unfriendly. After many years I have learned that they are not cold (*well, some are, but you find that everywhere*), and among friends they are very friendly. But becoming friends takes more than just five minutes here—more like five years, until the trust is built up to where you are finally let in the front door. And although we Americans may seem to be grossly superficial in comparison, I do believe that most American friendliness is genuine.

Since being spoken to by a stranger here in Germany is only a rare occasion, I am not used to it anymore when I visit the States, and it takes me a few days to readapt, which essentially means not freaking out when a stranger politely tries to open a conversation with me at the supermarket. I mean, that almost never happens in Germany, nor anywhere else in continental Europe for that matter. (Notice I left you Brits out of that one?)

A perfect example of the type of politeness that you get from Americans happened when I was running a half marathon in Providence, Rhode Island, one year. On my race belt, along with my start number, I had two gels tucked into the loops, enough to get me through the 21 kilometers. But at about kilometer 15 they were handing out gels—I mean, really overly ambitiously and amicably so that it would have been almost rude for someone not to take one. So I grabbed one and stuck it into my shorts for later use. Well, wouldn't you know that the helpers there who were handing out the packets were just so sweet that, to save us from the additional effort of opening those tricky gel packs, before they handed them over they already had them ripped open for us. Very sweet, no? NO! I obviously did not register this, and stuffing a gel packet, upside down no less, into my shorts was a very risky adventure. I was wondering why I was suddenly feeling sticky everywhere, and to top it off wouldn't you know the flavor was chocolate? I was in a very unpleasant predicament, but all I could do was laugh. We all know how tricky those gel packets can be to open sometimes, so of course I should have known the über-friendly aid station helpers would hold no bounds in supporting us.

Let's face it, the world is lacking such kindness and friendliness these days. Helping others. Giving back. Kindness is giving without expecting something in return. It is unselfish and humble, but despite its self-effacing nature, it is very respectable and powerful to witness or experience.

So, how can we be kind? That shouldn't be a difficult question to answer, but it is not as easy for most of us as it ought to be. Why not? Because we are so caught up in the details that we can't take in the whole picture. This is how running helps me—more specifically, long-distance running. I have the time to get down to nothingness. To clear my head of all my problems, to look into the forest when I hear a rustling in the leaves, or to enjoy the refreshing feeling of cool raindrops on my face. When we are free of those tiny little nagging details that have absolutely no relevance or major impact on our lives and those around us, then we can take the time to be a nicer person.

A few years ago, I made a conscious decision to be kinder to others simply by complementing them more. So often when I saw someone who has a new haircut, new clothes, have changed their style, or made a decision or taken action that I liked or impressed me, I used to acknowledge it internally but not say a word. Whether a member of my family, a friend, or a complete stranger, now I consciously relay all that positive information, and every single time I am rewarded with a smile. Even from those Germans.

The next step, after taking out the trash of my own mental burdens and becoming a kinder person, is helping others.

Running is a very selfish sport. It is not a team sport, unless you are in a relay race. And the physical and mental benefits of running are nontransferable, which makes it a perfect example of Freud's *id*, because you instantly want self-satisfaction. We are all guilty of this no matter what level of athlete we are.

I, for one, was (and still am, though to a lesser degree) one of the worst offenders, running because it made me feel good, kept my body in shape, and gave me an image boost when I landed on the podium. But after witnessing the bombings at the finish line of the 2013 Boston Marathon, I had an awakening. I felt a strong sense of guilt in the days and weeks following that event. All the victims had been spectators, simply there to applaud us runners on. I can remember distinctly running down Boylston Street toward the finish line and feeling the power that the fans were sending out with their claps and cheers as I ran by. They were really innocent victims and the "culprits," we runners, came out unscathed.

About five weeks after Boston, I happened to meet Armin and Alexandra Wolf at a swim seminar. We were a small group and got to talking during our lunch break. Of course, I knew who Armin Wolf was, the most well-known sports reporter in our area, for whom the baseball arena was named and who had recently, with his wife, established a running team that supported charity causes. Most of the runners on the team were really, really good, including a professional triathlete, the European mountain running champ, and the daughter of an Olympic medalist who was a top athlete in her own right. I had been in awe of the athletes since the inception of the team but hadn't really considered the philanthropic side until after Boston. I talked openly to Armin about my experience at the marathon, what I had witnessed, and how it had left me with a heavy burden.

He then asked me to join his team.

It is hard for me to describe the impact that this invitation had and still has on me. I was overjoyed at the chance to even meet some of the other athletes, though I knew that I was far from their level. But it also helped me to finally be able to give something back to others through my beloved hobby. It was no longer an *id* activity. It had transgressed to a *super-ego*. Let me just quickly clarify what the super-ego is with the help of Wikipedia, "The *super-ego* strives to act in a socially appropriate manner, whereas the *id* just wants instant self-gratification. The *super-ego* controls our sense of right and wrong and guilt. It helps us fit into society by getting us to act in socially acceptable ways." This action would subsequently help to induce balance in my life.

Not only did I start running with the team in races in which a donation was always made to a local charitable cause at each event, but the team started to volunteer their time to go into schools and help train and motivate kids to get more active, be healthy, and even get the kids to take part in races. At the time I didn't know to what degree this involvement would develop, whether I'd just be seen at events in the team jersey and smile for the photos or truly get inspired by its cause. But through the running team and Armin's influence in the media, I have been able to tell my stories. I've been asked to speak at corporate as well as sporting events, schools, and even on radio and local television, and each time it gives me the opportunity to motivate others to strive to reach their potential, whether it be running an ultra or simply living a healthier lifestyle.

Yes, I did get inspired by the team's cause and believe strongly in its mission.

And the best part of it all? My kids are proud to call me their mom.

Everyone has something inside of them to share, and everyone has more to give than they already do. It's just a matter of discovering the passion and finding the medium.

APPENDIX A

IRON DEFICIENCY IN DISTANCE RUNNERS

Just because it is the appendix, doesn't mean it is not part of the book...go ahead and read it!

In the winter of 2013, I was diagnosed with iron deficiency anemia. When I told this to my friends they said sarcastically, "Are you surprised?"

Actually, yes and no. Since I turned vegan I'd been eating healthier than any other time in my life. Breakfast is usually a kale smoothie, then come the grilled veggies with buckwheat, sweet potatoes, nuts, bean burgers, sorghum, almond or oatmeal milk, avocados, mangoes, and anything and everything that is colorful and fresh from my local vegetable market. I love to cook and enjoy spending time in the kitchen with my family. I snack on nuts, hummus, and veggie/bean salads. So, although I wasn't eating iron-loaded red meat, my diet was well-balanced and diverse; how could I possibly be lacking a vital nutrient?

Quite easily. And here are the three main reasons:

1. Diet: I eat no red meat, nor any other animal product.
2. Gender: I am female and lose blood monthly through menstruation.
3. Activity level: I run more than 50 miles per week.

I am sure that genetics plays a role here, too, but I blame my parents for too much as it is.

Several months before being diagnosed with anemia, I began to notice fatigue while training. After 10 kilometers at an easy pace, I'd be struggling to keep up with the group. Interval training times weren't where they should be, and then the clincher: my 10-kilometer race time seriously deteriorated.

Something was wrong. I knew it. I just wasn't sure what it was.

At first, I thought maybe my training needed to be revamped. More intervals? More speed? Fewer long runs? Is it simply my age? Then an acquaintance of mine suggested I get my iron levels tested. She had experienced a terrible iron deficiency that went undiagnosed for far too long, and it took her almost a year to get her levels back up to where they should be for an athlete that trains hard on a daily basis. She recommended getting my ferritin levels (not iron serum) checked, as ferritin is the protein which provides iron storage in the bloodstream.

In a nutshell, having adequate iron stores is essential to any endurance sport, as your ability to run (bike, swim, etc.) hinges on your capacity to get oxygen to your muscles, which is accomplished by your red blood cells. Red blood cells are made almost entirely of a protein called hemoglobin, and at the core of that protein is an iron atom. Oxygen binds to hemoglobin by binding with the iron atom at its center. Thus, if there isn't enough iron available to make red blood cells, there aren't enough red blood cells to carry oxygen to the muscles. And no oxygen means no high-level performance.

1. Diet

Iron is most readily absorbed from red meat, since it is already bound into a biologically available form called heme iron. Iron in vegetables, however, is more difficult to absorb because it is not bound in the "heme" form and is therefore called non-heme iron. Sources differ on the magnitude of this difference, but it is undisputedly significant. According to one study, about 8-16% of ingested iron will be absorbed if the source is heme iron (meat), while only 3-8% will be absorbed if the source is non-heme (vegetables and dairy). The numbers tend to vary widely because other factors can significantly influence iron absorption. For example, simultaneously consuming vitamin C can boost iron absorption by two- to tenfold, while calcium does the opposite and can actually reduce absorption by 50-60%.

2. Gender

Although it is possible for men to become iron deficient, the problem is much more often seen in women since they tend to eat less iron-containing foods than men and because they experience monthly menstruation. Studies have shown that as many as 20% of male, competitive, long-distance runners have low blood ferritin levels, while this number reaches 60-80% for female runners.

3. Activity Level

Why is an athlete more prone to iron deficiency than anyone else? Well, after a hard workout the body attempts to make new red blood cells by drawing iron from ferritin to create hemoglobin, and thus manufacture new red blood cells. But why does the body need to make more red blood cells after a workout? Because they are actually destroyed by hard training. The repeated trauma of forceful muscular contractions and foot strikes against the ground crush red blood cells, requiring new ones to be made. This situation can manifest as march hematuria, which occurs when blood is seen in the urine after repetitive impacts on the body, particularly affecting the feet. The word "march" is in reference to the condition arising in soldiers who have been marching for long periods. Hematuria can contribute to anemia, as it increases the iron turnover in an athlete, which is why they tend to need higher levels of stored iron than sedentary or moderately active people.

Another phenomenon is called Runner's Macrocytosis, manifesting in increased red blood cell size as a compensatory mechanism for increased red blood cell turnover. The impact forces from running can lead to red blood cell hemolysis and accelerate red blood cell production. This can shift the ratio of red blood cells toward younger, larger cells. This shift may be reflected in higher than normal MCV (mean corpuscular volume) values, an indicator of red blood cell size. This may indicate a propensity toward iron deficiency anemia due to high red blood cell turnover.

What does this all come down to? First, all endurance athletes should regularly get a blood test. Ask specifically to get your ferritin serum value checked as this is not part of the routine blood test. When I first went to my primary care doctor and said that I suspected iron deficiency anemia, he only tested my iron serum level, and, since I had already begun to take iron supplements, this level was very high because my blood was saturated. I was told to stop taking iron supplements. I wasn't convinced; thus, only after going to a doctor specializing in athlete health were my ferritin levels tested and my suspicions confirmed.

The next step is evaluating recommended values. As serum ferritin levels below 25 ng/mL are connected with performance drops and injury, levels above 50 ng/mL are recommended for both male and female athletes.

What now? Supplements. These come in many forms but can easily be taken in a tablet as iron salts: ferrous sulfate, ferrous fumarate, and ferrous gluconate. **Quantity and type should be determined under doctor's supervision.**

From what I've learned, even if I started eating red meat again, I would still require some level of iron supplements to continue at the same activity level. But for me, the health benefits of a diet based on plant products far outweigh any minor positive gain from eating meat. Thus, to maintain healthy iron levels, every endurance athlete should get their blood tested regularly and discuss with your doctor (preferably a sports specialist) to find out if or how much iron supplement is required.

Disclaimer: I am not a doctor nor expert on the subject of anemia by any means. And this topic is still under study with many conflicting opinions. My sources for this article are from Dr. Tim Noakes (*Lore of Running*), another blogger Tom Davis (*Running Writings*), Wikipedia, and of course, my own experience.

And many thanks to Valerie for tipping me off.

APPENDIX B

VACATION TRAINING TIPS FOR RUNNERS

Almost every hotel has a **fitness studio** with even the most basic of equipment. If they have a stationary bike or a treadmill, then you are all set. Personally, I can't run on a treadmill for much more than 30 minutes without going looney, but luckily there are lots of speed workouts you can do on one from 200- to 1000-meter intervals or a short warm-up and then a 5-kilometer tempo run. Use your imagination. If there are **weight machines,** then hop aboard and do some low-weight–high-rep lifting, which is perfect for runners. The muscles that are aching the next day are the ones that should get some future attention!

Even if you don't use the equipment, you can still get into your workout clothes and get down to the fitness studio and do some stretching, sit-ups, push-ups, core exercises, and before you know, it an hour has gone by. This is clearly more effective than if you try to slip in a few push-ups while waiting for your *significant other* to finish up in the bathroom.

If you want to go outside for a run but don't want to venture far for fear of getting lost (or the wrath of the family), then you can look for an incline and do some **hill work**. Sprint up, then jog or walk down. When sprinting up, concentrate on form—high knees, extended leg on the push-off. Or, there is always interval training for which you don't need much distance to run...yes, back and forth, back and forth may be boring, but just think how good that Mojito will taste poolside afterwards. Beach running is of course an incredible workout, although it tends more toward strength training than actual running, but who can't use that?

APPENDIX C

RECIPES

Now, what book on health and sports would be worth paying for if it doesn't contain a few healthy recipes in the end? Here are some of my favorites, all of which are vegan.

ROASTED CASHEW NUTS WITH SOY SAUCE

This is my absolute favorite snack and great for endurance athletes because it contains so much protein, fat, and salt!

Ingredients
- 2 ½ cups cashew nuts
- 4 Tbsp. soy sauce

Place the cashew nuts in pan (without any oil or fat!) and roast on medium heat for 45-60 minutes,

The endurance athlete's best friend: Roasted cashews with soy sauce

stirring often, until brown. Dark brown is fine, but don't let them burn! Then turn the stove off but leave the pan on the heat while pouring the soy sauce over the nuts. Stir nuts in the pan until the soy sauce is soaked into the nuts or cooked off and the pan is dry (about 1 minute). Let cool and store in a tin container for best results.

Kale Smoothies

In my opinion, kale is the best thing nature has to offer. I am always skeptical of fads, whether they be diet, exercise, nutrition, food, clothing, or hobbies, but this revolution of eating kale hits the bulls-eye in my book.

Kale is a typical cold-weather vegetable that is traditionally harvested after the first winter frost. It contains a significant amount of vitamins in high quantities, especially vitamin A,

Two massive kale plants

but also vitamin C, folic acid, potassium, magnesium, calcium, phosphorus, and, of course, iron. I'm sure if Popeye had known about kale, then spinach would have stayed in the can.

I buy the entire plant from my local farmer's market, and sometimes the plants are so large that I can only fit two at a time in the trunk of my car…and I have a big car.

I bring the plants home, lay them out on some newspaper on the living room floor, and let the kids separate the large parts of the stems before cutting the leaves into smaller pieces. I then blanch the leaves, let them air dry a bit, pack them in freezer bags in portions that last for three to four days, and into the freezer they go. I take out one bag at a time and leave it in the refrigerator to make my daily breakfast smoothies. Of course, you can also buy frozen kale, or buy it fresh and use it within a couple of days. You may find that you have a little trouble digesting the fresh leaves; if so, then simply blanch the leaves and chill…the leaves, not yourself, though a little chillin' is good for everyone.

I like the combination of pineapple with kale, and since it is important to combine iron-rich foods with those high in vitamin C in order to facilitate iron absorption, these two foods pair great. I usually toss in a mixture of nuts and seeds (macadamia, Brazil, and soy nuts, as well as pumpkin, chia, and flaxseeds, etc.), algae, coconut or oatmeal milk, and sometimes a plant-based protein powder, then whip it all together with a hand blender. But every day is different in terms of what I am craving and what I have in the house, so the ingredients are flexible. Ginger, lemon, kiwi, oranges, grapes, and a variety of other nuts have also made their appearances. It is simply a vitamin bomb, is actually really filling, and always makes me feel good afterwards.

ZUCCHINI-RIBBONS SALAD

Ingredients
- 2 medium zucchini
- 3 medium, juicy, ripe tomatoes
- 2 tablespoons walnut oil
- Salt & pepper to taste
- A couple of handfuls of toasted pumpkin seeds

Simply start off by using the ribbon accessory on your veggie spiralizer to cut the zucchini into long curly ribbons. Douse them with the walnut oil, salt, and pepper, and mix well. Arrange the zucchini in your serving dish. Dice the tomatoes and place them in a dollop in the middle of the zucchini ribbons. Then sprinkle toasted pumpkin seeds over it all!

Super easy and surprisingly delicious!

*Don't forget the pumpkin seeds! They make it special!

BLACK BEAN AND ROASTED SWEET POTATO BURGER

Ingredients

- 2 cups cooked black beans, mashed
- 2 cups sweet potatoes, peeled and cut into small cubes
- 2 tsp olive oil
- Salt/pepper
- One small yellow onion
- 2 tsp garlic
- 3 tsp tamari or soy sauce
- 2 tsp ground cumin
- 7 oz. cooked rice
- 1.5 tsp Worcestershire sauce
- 1 oz. cornmeal
- Oatmeal
- 3 shakes of cayenne pepper
- Cornmeal or toasted sesame seeds for coating

Preheat the oven to 350 °F (180 °C).

Spread out the sweet potato cubes onto a lightly oiled baking sheet and bake for about 20 minutes or until tender.

Cook the black beans and divide so that you have about a cup on reserve. The rest of the beans should be placed in a larger bowl and pureed.

Heat olive oil in a sauté pan and cook onion and garlic until slightly brown. Add them to the bowl of pureed beans, and add the soy sauce, cumin, Worcestershire, the rest of the whole beans, salt, and pepper. Gently fold in the cooked rice, sweet potatoes, oatmeal, and cornmeal.

At this point, if you want to freeze them, form the mixture into burgers and wrap tightly in plastic wrap.

Otherwise, form them into burgers, heat oil in a pan and cook burgers for 5 minutes on each side or until brown and slightly crispy.

Serve on a tortilla wrap with lettuce, tomato, avocado and mango chutney…or your favorite toppings.

MANGO CHUTNEY

Ingredients

- 3 large apples, peeled and roughly chopped
- 2 mangoes, peeled and cut into small pieces
- 1 red pepper, finely chopped
- 1 cup sugar (or less)
- One small onion, diced
- ¾ cup raisins
- ½ cup vinegar
- 1 Tbsp. finely chopped ginger
- 1 Tbsp. lemon juice
- 2 tsp curry powder
- ½ tsp each of nutmeg, cinnamon, and salt

Place the apples, mangoes, red pepper, sugar, onion, raisins, vinegar, and ginger in a saucepan and bring to a boil. Reduce the temperature and let simmer for 20 minutes, stirring occasionally, until the fruit is soft and begins to thicken. Then add the lemon juice, curry powder, nutmeg, cinnamon, and salt and cook for an additional 5 minutes.

Let cool before serving! Goes perfectly with those black bean burgers!